LOUIS C. TIFFANY'S
GLASS-BRONZES-LAMPS

LOUIS C. TIFFANY'S
GLASS-BRONZES-LAMPS

A Complete Collector's Guide

by Robert Koch

Crown Publishers, Inc.   New York

Library of Congress Catalog Card Number: 76-168327

ISBN: 0-517-505568

Printed in the United States of America

Designed by Margery Kronengold
and Hazel Rossbach

15 14 13 12 11 10 9 8

Dedicated to the hundreds of artists,
designers, and craftsmen
associated with the Tiffany organization
between 1878 and 1938

CONTENTS

ACKNOWLEDGMENTS

Since the publication in 1964 of the first edition of *Louis C. Tiffany, Rebel in Glass,* a great deal of new information has come to light. As a collector and dealer, I have gained greater confidence in authenticating and dating the many various products made under the supervision of the son of the founder of Tiffany and Company. Most of my research has been carried on in the shops and shows of the antiques market, and many dealers and collectors have been extremely cooperative and generous to me. To list all their names would be impossible. The following are mentioned because they were kind enough to provide some of the booklets, photographs, documents, or objects included in this collector's guide: Helen Eisenberg, Barry Friedman, Julius Gold, Gertrude Goodstein, Dorothy Gay Gordon, Harold Hindle, Jonathan Joseph, Walter Klein, Carol Macht, Eleanor Mulligan, the late Julia Sherman, the late James Stewart, and Mary Tuck. The book jacket was designed by Henry Gorsky and Irving Leviton; the manuscript was typed by Gloria Mansfield and edited by Kay Pinney. Above all, I owe an enormous debt of gratitude to my wife Gladys, without whom none of this would have been possible.

LOUIS C. TIFFANY'S
GLASS-BRONZES-LAMPS

ONE

LOUIS C. TIFFANY'S ENTERPRISES

A complete or definitive catalogue of the products of Tiffany Studios that would include all the objects associated with Louis C. Tiffany, the founder of the firm, can never be compiled. The extraordinarily prolific character of this artist and designer, described in detail in his biography, *Rebel in Glass,* led him to venture into a very wide variety of materials and media and to employ many other artists and designers to carry out his ideas.

Tiffany, the son of the founder of the famed Fifth Avenue Tiffany and Company, began his career as a painter shortly after the Civil War, and the production of objects employing his concepts of beauty continued for five years after his death in 1933. During this span of more than seventy years of productivity, his most important work was rendered in glass, much of which has been accidentally lost or damaged, if not wantonly destroyed. It has been estimated that half the church windows made under his supervision no longer exist. Of the vases and

1. Louis C. Tiffany.

lamps, the percentage may be even higher, although they keep appearing on the market after having been hidden away for many years.

The recent revival of interest in Tiffany items has had a number of interesting consequences. Dealers who hitherto rejected any Tiffany product as not old enough are now eagerly searching for "sleepers," and collectors competing for rare types are forcing the prices into a continuous rise. Rare and unusual vases of Favrile glass, particularly those of red glass or paperweight technique, and the more intricate leaded glass lampshades are now bringing prices in four or even five figures. Many examples of this type are illustrated in *Rebel in Glass.* They are beyond the reach of the ordinary or beginning collector, and are therefore not featured in this volume. Furthermore, it is still not feasible to select all the finest-quality specimens of Tiffany's work from the many private collections, for display in photographs. Such a display would require superb color plates and would be useful primarily as an art book, a project not to be undertaken until all the facts have come to light. This book, therefore, presents many of the products and types of objects that were made in quantity and have not been previously published, except in the scarce booklets and catalogues issued by Tiffany Studios for promotion at their retail sales outlets.

Quality, uniqueness, and originality were always stressed by Tiffany as important aspects of his work. In a booklet published in 1901, simply entitled "Tiffany Studios," the aims were described as follows:

There is among people of educated taste an increasing demand for craftsmanship possessing purity of design and stability of construction, which are the essential elements of enduring worth. The advantage of surrounding ourselves in our homes, in our churches, and in our public buildings with objects of intrinsic merit hardly needs to be urged. Apart from the conscious pleasure and the unconscious education which such surroundings afford, there is the economic gain of permanence, achieved through careful workmanship, and through the fact that handicraft which possesses beauty and originality is independent of passing fashion. We see this in the many admirable pieces of work which have come down to us from former times and are now doing service for a third or fourth generation of owners.

There are not, however, enough antiques to meet our requirements, and if there were, the craftsmanship of one century could not entirely satisfy the needs of the next, so the art-worker of today chooses for study the best types of former times, and from these evolves others which show the distinctive character of his own epoch and the impress of his own thought. The Tiffany Studios have achieved marked success in this creative craftsmanship, and have accomplished a great variety of artistic work, ranging from the design and production of a single object of art to the decoration of an entire house.

Some idea of the scope of this work may be gained in the exhibition rooms of the studios. Sketches and designs for the treatment of walls, ceilings and woodwork of house interiors may be seen there, together with examples of the correct use of relief and plaster work, and the adaptability of paints and paperings and of tapestries and other textile fabrics.

In the selection of hangings for curtains and portieres—a difficult problem since large masses of color must necessarily be used—careful study of the surroundings is made and special fabrics provided when occasion requires.

The Tiffany Studios have been eminently successful in designing special carpetings, and in selecting the products of the best looms. In addition to these, their collection of Oriental rugs, constantly renewed by choice examples of the art of Eastern weavers enables them to fulfill the requirements of every condition.

There is exhibited at the showroom a wide range of styles in movable furniture, including carefully chosen specimens of the antique, conscientious reproductions, and original pieces having all the qualities of form and color, construction and finish required for purposes of utility and for harmony with their surroundings.

An important part of the work of the studios is the artistic treatment of artificial light. They produce not only lamps and candlesticks of unusual interest and beauty, but design fixtures for the installation of gas and electricity. The distinctive features of these lamps and fixtures is the use of Favrile Glass and the color-finishing of the metal work, which brings it into proper relation with the furniture and decoration surrounding it.

Glass mosaic, a very beautiful and permanent form of decoration, and one in which the Studios have produced many notable works, is appropriately applied to the enrichment of walls and ceilings and to mantel facings. Examples of its use in these and other ways may be seen in the showrooms.

Of Favrile glass there is a large and specially attractive collection of vases, jars, vinaigrettes, table glasses, globes and shades. The distinctive decorative qualities of this ware, and its almost limitless range of color effects adapt it perfectly to decorative purposes, and to those uses where a union of utilitarian qualities and artistic effect is desired. Many of the individual pieces have unusual interest for the collector.

The nature and scope of the business at this time is readily seen in an ad that appeared in "The International Studio" in 1902 (see Ill. 2). The founder and director of Tiffany Studios was then fifty-four years of age, a successful artist and a businessman of international renown.

The name "Tiffany Studios" was first used in 1900, and therefore any article so inscribed must have been made in the twentieth century. However, the business was then already more than twenty years old and had been reorganized several times. The earliest name, from 1879 until 1885, was "Louis C. Tiffany and Co., Associated Artists"; next, from 1885 until 1892, it was "Tiffany Glass Co." From 1892 until 1900, it was "Tiffany Glass and Decorating Co." Another name used between 1900 and 1902 was "Allied Arts Co.," mostly in connection with the production of furniture for Tiffany Studios. Objects marked with both the monogram "T.G. & D. Co." and the words "Tiffany Studios" were produced between 1898 and 1902.

Prior to 1890, Tiffany's products were intended for individual rather than mass consumption. Therefore no advertisements or price catalogues were needed. During the nineties only six pieces of promotional mate-

2. Advertisement for Tiffany Studios in March 1902.

rial were issued. The first was a booklet distributed at the Chicago Fair of 1893. In 1896 three very small booklets were made up on windows, mosaics, and Favrile glass; in 1897 a partial list of church windows was printed; and in 1898 the first lamps were promoted. However, the vast majority of the items now being sought by collectors were made during the first quarter of the twentieth century. Descriptive booklets and price catalogues were made up by both Tiffany Studios and Tiffany and Co., and these clearly show the diversity of the products and will help the collector to identify them properly.

The word "Favrile" is a Tiffany creation—it can apply to all objects produced under his direct supervision. It was registered with the U.S. Patent Office as part of a trademark on November 13, 1894, with the claim that it had been used since February 1892. "Favrile" does not, as has sometimes been claimed, originate from the German word for color, but it does derive from the old English "Fabrile" meaning "handmade," with the same root as "fabricate." A few of the oldest original paper labels on Tiffany glass from 1892 show that the proper spelling, Fabrile, was used at first, but this was changed to Favrile to create a unique word for the trademark of the Tiffany Glass and Decorating Company.

Favrile was first used for glass blown at the Tiffany plant in Corona, New York. A booklet entitled "Tiffany Favrile Glass" was issued in 1896. Two years later another booklet was issued to introduce "Tiffany Favrile Glass-Lamps." In 1902 when the name of the firm was officially changed to Tiffany Studios, the new trademark used Favrile to apply to decorative glass, enamels, and pottery. The further broadening of the meaning of the term for use with all metal as well as glass and ceramic items can be found in the *Blue Books* issued annually from 1902 until 1916 by the Fifth Avenue Tiffany and Company. In the *Blue Book* for 1911, Louis C. Tiffany's Favrile glass-lamps are described as "unique forms and color effects in combinations of Favrile glass with bronze metal mountings and leaded or blown Favrile glass shades," and Tiffany Studios desk sets are listed as "Tiffany Favrile glass and Etched metal." In 1919 the trademark with the word Favrile was taken over by A. Douglas Nash and used until 1928 for all the products, regardless of material, produced at the Louis C. Tiffany Furnaces under Nash's direction.

Favrile as a term is most frequently applied to glass, but it does not imply any particular kind of glass except that which was made or worked by the Tiffany organization. The use of Favrile for Tiffany Studios desk sets made of Tiffany metal without glass or enamels is

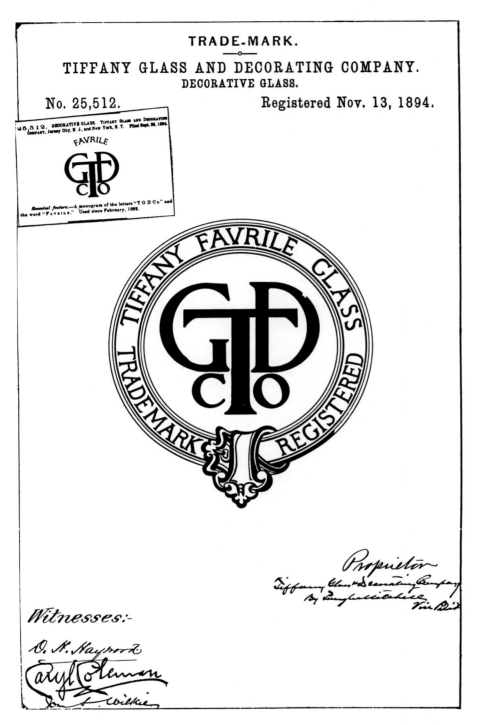

3. Trademark of the Tiffany Glass and Decorating Company in use for the ten years between 1892 and 1902.

less frequent but not without precedent. In essence, it merely means handmade by craftsmen under the supervision of Louis C. Tiffany or his associates.

Louis C. Tiffany was one of the first and most prolific collectors in America. At a time when many of his very wealthy clients, like the Vanderbilts and the Havemeyers, began to buy European paintings, Tiffany was one of several American decorators who began to collect decorative objects for their qualities of both beauty and craftsmanship. These decorators also made it a point to introduce such objects into the homes they decorated, and thereby they initiated the vogue for collecting antiques and decorative objects that has continued and increased ever since the mid-nineteenth century.

In 1878, when he was only thirty years of age, Tiffany had already collected the first outstanding group of Japanese sword guards in any private collection in the United States. His closest friend and collaborator, the painter Samuel Colman, collected Chinese textiles and porcelain; his associate, Lockwood de Forest, collected East Indian carvings; his father's associate at Tiffany and Company, Edward C. Moore, had a remarkable group of Persian glass and metalwork; and another friend of the Tiffany family, J. Taylor Johnston, first president of the Metropolitan Museum of Art, was busy gathering the first and one of the finest collections of American Colonial furniture. Many items from these early collections soon found their way into New York's Metropolitan Museum of Art. Less than twenty years later, in 1896, glass designed by Louis C. Tiffany was added to the permanent collection of this museum.

Throughout his long and productive career, in all the items that he designed and that were produced under his direct supervision, Tiffany always kept in mind the needs and desires of the true collector. Quality of craftsmanship and durability, even in the most fragile materials, were always prime considerations for his products, which were all intended to be treasured by their owners and to outlast the generation that saw them for the first time. They were designed to be used first as gifts, then to become heirlooms, and eventually to achieve the status of prized antiques. Since the first piece of Tiffany glass or metal appeared on the market, many such items have fulfilled the first two of these aims and will certainly eventually realize the third one.

Basically, two types of objects were made by Louis C. Tiffany or under the auspices of the several firms established by him: unique items such as the paintings by his own hand and one-of-a-kind articles of metal or glass; and articles duplicated and made in quantity that were intended to be matched and combined with one another, such as table settings and desk sets. Most of the items in the first category are now in museums or in the hands of advanced collectors.

Like any great work of art, whether it is a painting by Rembrandt or a saltcellar by Cellini, a unique piece of Tiffany must have its value established by the prices paid at auction. These vary according to the tastes of the times, but it is unlikely that hitherto unknown superior pieces of Tiffany glass will suddenly appear in the shops of any but the most informed dealers. If a few such pieces still remain in hiding, they will probably not gather dust much longer for there are now too many people on the lookout for "sleepers" in Tiffany glass. The unique or "very rare" examples are already bringing high prices. There is no reason to believe that this situation will change. Tiffany's work has been belatedly recognized, and fine examples of his craftsmanship are now generally accepted as works of art.

Tiffany, however, was more than an artist; he was also an industrial designer. As a designer and promoter, he supervised the production of thousands of art objects that were distributed all over the world. During his lifetime (1848–1933), he saw a shift in taste from the opulent Victorian to the austere Modern, and he himself became a leading spokesman for the Art Nouveau style.

TWO

TIFFANY'S PAINTINGS AND SKETCHES

Louis C. Tiffany was a prolific painter, but as yet his contributions in this area of the fine arts are very little known and have not been adequately evaluated. There has never been a retrospective show of Tiffany paintings, an event that is long overdue.

Before he was anything else, Tiffany was first and always a painter of landscapes. He left school at seventeen years of age to study with George Inness in his New York studio. Two years later, in 1867, one of his paintings was accepted for inclusion in the 42nd Annual Exhibition of the National Academy of Design. By 1892 this institution had shown thirty-five oil paintings by Tiffany in its successive annuals. These were listed in their catalogues for prices ranging from $200 to $3,500. Between 1872 and 1879, Tiffany also showed another thirty-five paintings, without duplication, at the monthly exhibitions at the Century Club in New York. Many of these pictures were watercolors. In 1870 he was the youngest member ever to be elected to the Century Club, and the following year he became an associate member of the National Academy.

At the Philadelphia Centennial Exposition in 1876, Tiffany showed three oils and six watercolors, mostly of subjects from North Africa. Several of these were then already in private collections. In 1878 two oil paintings by Tiffany were shown in Paris at the Exposition Universelle, and in 1893 five Tiffany paintings were included in Chicago's World Columbian Exposition show of watercolors.

In February 1916, Tiffany Studios exhibited eighty-two paintings by their founder and president, all completed before 1900. Of these, I know the present location of only about one-third. Some are now in museums, including the Metropolitan Museum of Art, the Brooklyn Museum, and the Yale Art Gallery; others are owned by Tiffany's descendants, and the rest are in private collections.

4. Louis C. Tiffany, "Pushing Off the Boat," oil on canvas, 1887.

Tiffany never stopped painting. In 1908, on a trip up the Nile, he made many watercolor sketches from the deck of his yacht, and when he retired in 1919, he spent much of his time during the summer months at Laurelton Hall painting flowers in his gardens. He loved nature in all its forms, and he encouraged his intimates and guests to try their hands at painting.

All Tiffany's finished paintings are signed, but many of his sketches are not. His earliest signature, as a student, was "L. Tiffany." This was soon replaced by the "Louis C. Tiffany," which was his signature most of his life. Small paintings may bear only the initials L.C.T. Very few of his paintings are dated, and sometimes he added the date many years after a painting had been completed. Not all these dates added by Tiffany himself are accurate—he had a poor memory for figures and dates, and no accurate account was ever kept of his paintings.

5. Watercolor design for a window, signed by Louis C. Tiffany. Author's Collection.

As a painter, Tiffany ranks as a prominent member of the last generation of the Hudson River School of American landscape painters. His scenes of Arabs in North Africa are most popular among collectors, but his Brittany scenes run a close second. All his work has a strong decorative quality, although in figural composition he sometimes shows a weakness in anatomy. He was well aware of this weakness, and for that reason depended on others for the designs of many of his figure windows.

A signed Tiffany watercolor of a courtyard, 21 by 15 inches, sold at auction in New York in April 1971 for $800. Normally, his oil paintings bring higher prices than his watercolors.

Tiffany's ability as a painter made it possible for him to create many of his own designs for important windows. One example exists of a full-size cartoon, oil on canvas, by Tiffany's own hand for the very large "Education" figure window at Yale University (see *Rebel in Glass,* pages 103 and 104). There are also a great many renderings for windows that have only an inscription—"Approved by Louis C. Tiffany"—written in pencil on the mat. Most of these are the work of draftsmen employed by Tiffany Studios. Such designs, which were consistent with the principles advocated by Tiffany and were actually approved by him, are just as prized by most collectors as any other product of Tiffany's workshops. This is also true of the designs of Tiffany interiors, a few of which have survived. However, the value of such renderings usually depends on their decorative effects rather than on historical importance. The style and character of any such items can best be checked by comparing them with photos of windows and interiors reproduced in *Rebel in Glass.*

THREE

PRESSED GLASS FOR TILES AND JEWELS

According to a statement in a Tiffany booklet published in 1896, it was in 1872 that "experiments in glass-making were instituted in New York, followed by valuable discoveries . . . which ultimately led to the invention of Tiffany Favrile glass." These were experiments conducted at the Heidt glasshouse in Brooklyn where a Venetian glassman, Andrea Boldini, who had been trained at the Salviati Glass Factory in Murano, was foreman of the plant. Both John LaFarge and Louis C. Tiffany studied the chemistry and techniques of glassmaking as pupils of Boldini.

In the fall of 1878, Tiffany launched his first business venture. This was Louis C. Tiffany & Co., Associated Artists. The "associates"—the group included Samuel Colman, Lockwood de Forest, and Candace Wheeler—accepted Tiffany's leadership, and decorated many interiors with Tiffany-fabricated and Tiffany-inspired accessories, only a few of which have survived. The only objects the firm produced in quantity that are collectible today are the glass tiles made for use in screens and sconces and for trim on fireplaces or walls. A fine 1880 installation of Tiffany glass tiles can be seen around the great fireplace in the Veterans' Room of the Seventh Regiment Armory in New York. (See illustration in *Rebel in Glass,* page 37.)

Such Tiffany glass tiles were made of "pot metal" glass usually poured into open molds. Various colors and consistencies of opalescent glass were blended in the molten state and then poured to achieve a swirl effect in each tile. The molds were squares one, two, three, or four inches to the side and at most a half-inch deep. There were several patterns, including the five-petal rosette, dragon, Chinese design, jewel, and random punch. The last was an effect produced in the glass after it had been removed from the mold but was not yet completely hardened. Many of the square three-inch tiles have the inscription "Pat. Feb. 8th 1881 L.C.T. & Co." The larger four-inch tiles were difficult to mount because of their weight and the smooth surfaces of the glass. Many of these simply bear the words "Patent Applied For," since none of the various methods Tiffany tried for holding them firmly in place worked effectively. During the eighties a great number of these tiles were made at the Heidt glasshouse in Brooklyn. Glass tiles were an important feature of many of the interiors decorated by Tiffany; a large number were sold on the open market, and still a great many more have come down to the present without ever having been used in an installation. In 1957 a furniture designer, Edward Wormley, introduced a line of tables for the Dunbar Furniture Company featuring inlaid Tiffany tiles.

Thus, Tiffany tiles can still be purchased, and many are extremely attractive because of the free blending of glass of various tones and colors. Some were also treated with a metallic iridescence that later became characteristic of much of Tiffany's glass. One admirer of these tiles believes that they are the true genesis of American abstract painting. Although this idea may be somewhat farfetched, there is without doubt a superficial resemblance between some of the Tiffany tiles and paintings on a much larger scale done in recent years.

Some glass tiles have turned up with the name "Louis C. Tiffany" etched along the narrow edge of the glass. It has been impossible to determine whether or not this inscription was on the tiles originally. There is also a story, which may or may not be myth, that in every Tiffany installation the tile in the upper right-hand corner was so inscribed. Whether this is true or not, the tiles so marked apparently are no different from those simply impressed with the "Patent Applied For" mark. All Tiffany tiles, even the unmarked ones, are easy to au-

6. The big glass press at Tiffany Furnaces in Corona, New York.

thenticate since, unlike most other Tiffany products, they were never imitated.

After 1892, when Tiffany established his own plant in Corona, he continued to have his workmen make tiles from the old molds but he also developed many new sizes and shapes. There were three glass presses at Corona. One was a small table model that came from Sandwich, for very small molds used to make glass jewels less than three inches long. A medium-size press was used for ordinary three- and four-inch tiles, and a large press was used to develop new forms and types. With the expansion in the range of objects made at Tiffany's, the uses for pressed glass jewels and tiles were greatly increased. Special shapes were introduced for lamps and lighting fixtures; most interesting of these were the "turtleback" tiles in gold, green, blue, and red iridescent glass. Also iridescent, in a variety of lengths and widths, were the prisms meant to hang from the outer rims of Tiffany lampshades.

In 1971, Tiffany glass tiles could be bought at various prices depending on their color and condition. Small (three-inch) ones might be bought as low as $5.00 if they were without iridescence, but the price rises sharply for an iridescent tile or one with unusual color. The most desirable, the iridescent turtleback tile, may bring more than $100. Gold

7. Sample panel of twelve three-inch early Tiffany glass tiles, none of which is iridescent.

8. Nine four-inch Tiffany glass tiles, all of which have some iridescence.

9. Six four-inch and four three-inch Tiffany tiles showing a variety of the rough or uneven surfaces created to help in mounting the glass.

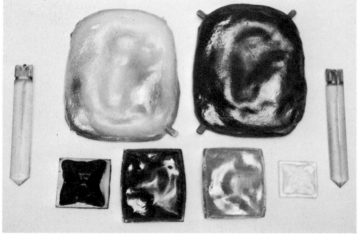

10. Two turtlebacks, two prisms, and four large jewels, all of Tiffany pressed iridescent glass.

11. Tiffany hanging fixture using turtleback tiles. *Tiffany Studios Photograph, courtesy of Mary Tuck.*

is the most common color; blue, being scarcer, would command a higher price. Red is so scarce that it is hardly ever seen for sale.

Iridescent glass scarab beetles were pressed from circular molds, each of which produced several different sizes of beetle, which then had to be cut out from the disc after it had completely cooled. The scarab has been a symbol of luck and longevity since the time of the ancient Egyptians. Real beetles are often iridescent in color; but as far as is now known, the only iridescent glass scarab beetles are those made by Tiffany. None of these is ever signed or marked on the glass, but that does not matter—it is not likely that they will be reproduced.

Glass scarabs were used at Tiffany Studios as color accents on lamp bases or, on rare occasions, on bronze pottery. Most frequently, however, they were set in 18-karat gold by jewelers at Tiffany and Company, to be used as stickpins, studs, cuff links, necklaces, and the like. The Tiffany and Company *Blue Book* catalogue of 1911, on pages 612 and 613, lists "Tiffany Favrile Beetle Jewelry" mounted in 18-karat gold in twelve different items ranging from pendants at $2.50 each to lavalieres at $225 each. These items, when in their original mountings, are all marked "Tiffany and Company."

14. Tiffany desk lamp with five-inch iridescent glass beetle as a shade.

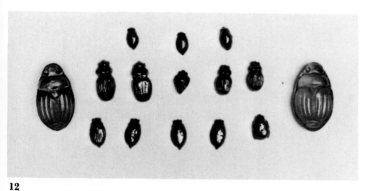

12

13

12. Tiffany glass scarab beetles of various sizes.

13. Tiffany glass seal in the shape of three scarab beetles.

Recently, loose Tiffany scarab beetles have been set in modern mountings of 14-karat gold or sterling silver. These are not marked or signed in any way but are very popular, since there is no doubt about the authenticity of the glass. Three such rings sold at auction in January 1971 for $150, as a lot. Scarabs in original mounts are much more valuable. Also in beetle form are the Tiffany pressed glass seals and the large (five-inch-long) scarabs for either small lampshades or paperweights, as shown in Ills. 13 and 14.

15. Blue iridescent Tiffany glass jewel in original Tiffany and Company mounting, marked "Tiffany & Co."

17. Three lampshades using panels of "Favrilefabrique" glass. *Tiffany Studios Photograph.*

16. Blue Tiffany iridescent pressed glass jewel mounted as a pendant.

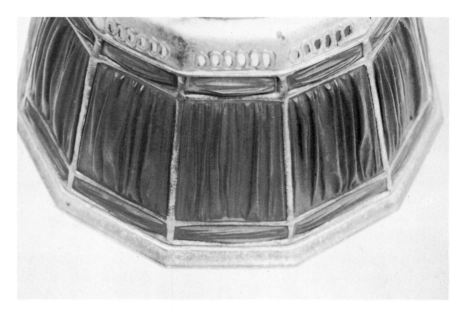

18. Detail of shade with "Favrilefabrique." *Tiffany Studios Photograph.*

Many other shapes for glass jewels were made, most of them in smaller quantities than scarabs. Some were designed specifically for use as jewelry (Ill. 15), but others had several different applications. The pendant shown in Ill. 16 was also used to decorate the handle of a bronze paper knife.

In 1913 a new kind of pressed glass was developed that has been called by several names, including "Favrilefabrique" or "Tiffany linen-fold" glass. This glass, which imitated fabric, was used exclusively for lampshades (see Ills. 17, 18, and 19). The method for pressing or casting a complete circle of glass like that in Ill. 19 was a contribution of Leslie H. Nash, son of the first foreman of the Corona Tiffany glasshouse.

The Victory Medallion 1918 (Ill. 20) was one of the last innovations in Tiffany Favrile pressed glass. By then the vogue for iridescence had begun to wane.

In the revival of American Art Nouveau and Tiffany Favrile glass, tiles and pressed glass occupied a prominent position right from the start. When, in October 1957, *House Beautiful* featured an article on "Iridescence," Tiffany tiles were included both on the cover and in the illustrations inside. Today most representative collections of American glass include some Tiffany tiles. They are relatively plentiful and therefore inexpensive, and are an excellent way for a beginning collector to study the colors and qualities of Tiffany glass. Only by careful study of this kind can he gain the confidence to invest in the rarer and more expensive items.

19. Shade made completely of Tiffany "Fabrique" glass as patented by Leslie Nash.

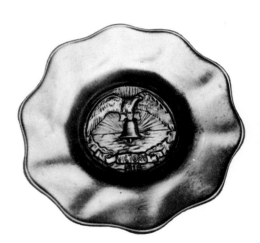

20. Victory 1918 pressed iridescent glass medallion mounted in blown glass dish.

21. Samples of tiles were on display in a false fireplace at Tiffany Furnaces in Corona.

FOUR

CATHEDRAL GLASS FOR WINDOWS AND MOSAICS

Louis C. Tiffany designed and made his first figure window in 1878. The glass, a new kind of American opalescent window glass, also came from the same Heidt glasshouse where Tiffany made his first tiles. The idea of using opalescent glass for pictorial windows seems to have originated in either New York or New England in the 1870s. Patents issued to Tiffany in 1881 prove that he was one of the first to employ several new methods in using this kind of window or "cathedral" glass early in his career.

From the very first, stained-glass windows were regarded by Tiffany as a form of painting—and they may still be considered as such. Large windows, like large paintings, require a large space and usually find their way into public collections. Rollins College in Winter Park, Florida, thanks to the efforts of Hugh F. McKean, has the finest collection of Tiffany windows in the world. There it is possible to study the various kinds of glass, and how it was cut and leaded into the finest decorative windows ever produced in this country, equal and sometimes superior to the best European efforts in this medium. It is certainly

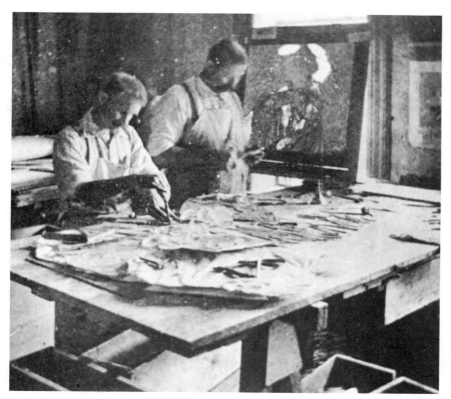

22. Cutting Favrile glass in 1896.

23. Henry Salzer, designer in the mosaic department of Tiffany Studios.

worth a trip to Florida to see this collection. Photographs, even in color, cannot do these windows justice.

Like paintings, windows can be classified by subject matter though it has no relationship to their quality or value. The majority of surviving Tiffany windows are religious in theme and were made as memorials for installation in churches. Many of these were designed by artists other than Tiffany. In a Tiffany booklet of 1896, in addition to the "Resurrection" painting by Tiffany, there are designs by Edward P. Sperry, J. A. Holzer, Joseph Lauber, and Frederick Wilson. There is also a photograph entitled "cutting Favrile glass," showing that the trademark name was also applied to window or cathedral glass. From 1892 this glass was made in Tiffany's Furnaces at Corona, New York, where there was always at least one cathedral glass shop and one blowing glass shop. The following is a statement from the booklet of 1896:

Our windows are made of Tiffany Favrile Glass which is produced exclusively at our furnaces and cannot be obtained from other makers, or used by other artists. In range, depth and brilliancy of color it has never been equaled, and when we employ it in window work the greatest care is exercised in selecting the piece in order that we may attain the desired effect both in color and texture. The selection is made by a trained artisan, who may be either a man or a woman, according to their fitness for the especial work in hand, but always under the supervision of an artist.

As all our windows are built in accordance with the mosaic theory, without the intervention of paint, stains, or enamels, they are practically indestructible and will not corrode, peel or fade.

Windows installed in public buildings or churches were usually signed on the glass in the lower right-hand corner. Those made before 1892 were inscribed "Tiffany Glass Company, New York"; then for a decade the word "Decorating" was inserted, and finally, after 1902, "Tiffany Studios, New York" was used. Occasionally a very fine landscape window was signed simply "Louis C. Tiffany" in block capital letters.

Windows made for private homes were never signed or inscribed in any way, on the assumption that the owner would always be there to attribute the makers. It is these windows that are most often a matter of controversy. There is no way to tell by looking at the glass alone whether or not a window is a true Tiffany product. Many other makers could duplicate most types of Tiffany window glass, and those that were too difficult to make could be purchased on the open market. Unsigned windows, like unsigned paintings, are always a challenge to the connoisseur unless there is documentary evidence at their source.

Larger windows can sometimes be cut apart and sections of special interest, such as landscapes, flowers, or decorative elements, can be mounted as separate units. Tiffany himself did just this with his "Four Seasons" window when he installed it inside his own home at Oyster Bay. Repairs to minor breaks or the replacement of a few pieces of glass are possible with only very little change in the general effect. It is difficult, of course, to find craftsmen or artisans as skilled as those trained and supervised by Tiffany, but there are glass studios in many major cities that can handle most jobs of this kind. They often have to repair or make new windows for churches, and some even have a stock of old glass that can be used to replace broken or missing pieces of a Tiffany window. Such repairs or replacements can usually be detected on very close examination, and they do affect the value of the window. The same is true, and even more important, with regard to repairs to leaded glass lampshades, often the work of the same craftsmen who made windows and mosaics.

24. Joseph Lauber, "An Angel of Praise," 1894, for a Tiffany window.

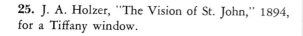

25. J. A. Holzer, "The Vision of St. John," 1894, for a Tiffany window.

26. Frederick Wilson, "The Ascension," 1894, for a Tiffany window.

25   26

27. Tiffany glass screen, 1902.

28. Dragonfly pendant for a lamp, made at Tiffany Studios. These pendants measure 10¼ by 6½ inches.

29. Mosaic disc of 1902. Author's Collection.

Tiffany, always conscious of the collector, also made sample panels and small windows that lend themselves to any kind of setting without alteration. An example is the panel he presented to his father and mother in 1891 on the occasion of their golden wedding anniversary. It measures only 21¾ inches by by 26¼ inches. For his oldest daughter, he made a landscape panel with irises, 30 inches by 18 inches, which was very attractively mounted in a window of the suburban home of one of his grandsons. As mentioned earlier, Louis C. Tiffany considered the stained-glass window a form of painting, and it can still be considered as such and treated accordingly by the collector.

Also sought by collectors are the sample panels made by Tiffany Studios to show the various designs possible in lampshades. These measure about 12 by 18 inches and readily lend themselves to a variety of decorative uses. Equally decorative are the leaded glass butterflies and the dragonfly pendants that were meant to be hung by chains from the rim of large lampshades. Very few of these are signed or

30. The entrance to the United States pavilion at the Paris World's Fair in 1900 displayed two Tiffany windows, the "Four Seasons" and the "River of Life."

marked in any way, but they can often be identified when they match the design and workmanship of a Tiffany lamp.

When mosaics are installed in a building, they become part of a wall, and so are even more of a problem to transport than windows. But, again, samples exist that can be found. Tiffany Studios made up a few copper discs 7¼ inches in diameter, into which mosaics were mounted. These are usually marked "Tiffany Studios" on the copper backing. One of a dragonfly is shown in Ill. 29.

Mosaics were also used as decorative surfaces on lamps, inkwells, and other objects made for use in the home. The tesserae were all made of glass, and very often the same iridescent quality was achieved that characterized other forms of Tiffany glass. But Tiffany glass does not need to be iridescent to be genuine. Tiffany and the men who worked for him used just about every formula for glass that was known to them. Although most famed for opalescent and iridescent glass, Tiffany Glass Company and its successors made many products that did not use any special effects. Tiffany mosaics, for instance, in some cases do not appear to have any quality other than that their design makes them different from the mosaics made in Italy today.

FIVE

BLOWN GLASS FOR VASES AND BOWLS

For more than thirty-five years, from 1892 until 1928, free-blown glass was produced at the Tiffany Furnaces in Corona, New York. The production fell into three periods: the early period, 1892 to 1900, when experimentation and variety of shapes and colors dominated; the peak period, between 1900 and 1918, when the greatest quantities of items were produced; and the late, or Nash, period, from 1918 to 1928, when pastel colors were featured.

It was while preparing the chapel for the Columbian Exposition in Chicago that Louis C. Tiffany felt the need to have his own blown glass. At that time he himself had fifteen years' experience at making tiles, windows, and mosaics, but it was a fortunate meeting with Arthur J. Nash that made possible the realization of Tiffany's desire to produce blown glass. Nash had just arrived from England, where he had been a manager for one of the Thomas Webb glasshouses in Stourbridge. The two men decided to work together, and formed a corporation that was later to become Tiffany Furnaces. The first shop was set up in a building that had formerly held a laundry.

Details of the history of the Tiffany glasshouse were given to me in a series of interviews with the late Jimmy Stewart, one of which comprises the following chapter. Unfortunately, knowing the names of the gaffers has not helped to identify the work of each. Stewart's sketchbook, also illustrated here, is much more help in this respect.

Tom Manderson, who came from Philadelphia where he had worked for Gillinder Glass, was the first master blower (or gaffer) at Tiffany's. It was Manderson who introduced the flower form, the pyroform, and the jack-in-the-pulpit vases that remained popular as shapes even after he himself left Corona. But these were not the only shapes made. Every possible variety of size and shape of vase or bowl was turned out at one time or another at Tiffany's. There were so many variations they almost defy classification. In a booklet published by the Tiffany Glass and Decorating Company in 1898, some of the shapes were described as follows:

The forms of Tiffany Favrile Glass are very largely derived from natural motives. . . . Tiffany Favrile glass is also made in the following forms: Partingeaux, Cantharus, Lecythus, Amphora, Pelike, Buire, Ewer, Tazza, etc.

Louis C. Tiffany was always the designer; Arthur J. Nash was the plant manager. None of the Tiffany original designs for blown glass have survived, although some must have existed, as is proved by a well-worn rubber stamp meant to be used on such drawings. A former employee has explained that Tiffany made his sketches in pencil on any old scrap of paper that happened to be handy. These were traced and then rendered by one of the artist-draftsmen hired for the purpose. Tiffany would approve the finished drawing by signing, in pencil, in the space provided by the rubber stamp.

On September 26, 1894, the Tiffany Glass and Decorating Company filed its application to register the "Favrile" trademark that had been in use since February 1892. The wording, which described window glass as much as blown glass, referred to "colored or stained glass windows, mosaics, glassware or glass used in conjunction with other substances in manufacture or the arts." Included were such terms as "fabric glass, sunset glass, horizon glass, twig glass and lace glass," all of which were used in various windows and to all of which the term "Favrile" applies. The use of Favrile, meaning "handmade," for all the forms of glass made and used by Tiffany craftsmen was intended simply as a guarantee to his customers and to future collectors that the glass was of the finest quality.

The earliest reliably documented piece of blown Tiffany glass is a green marbleized rose bowl with gold thread overlay that the Musée des Arts Décoratifs of the Louvre purchased in Paris from S. Bing on June 2, 1894.

Most of the early pieces from 1892 to 1895 were marked only by the application of a paper label. Unless a particular vase can be traced to a source prior to 1900, these paper labels are not reliable for identification. They are too easily transferred.

Identification of the early unmarked ware is extremely difficult. These pieces were the production of an experimental phase of the blown glass project, and the master craftsman, Tom Manderson, was a highly versatile gaffer. He not only blew glass into traditional shapes, but evolved many new shapes and forms that, although they were unique at the time, have frequently been copied since. The foreman, Arthur J. Nash, encouraged the workmen to learn the full range of English and Venetian types, but the boss, Louis C. Tiffany, then often criticized them by his repeated comment: "Too much Stourbridge." He wanted, above all else, free creativity and new organic qualities emerging from the inherent nature of the glass itself.

The results can be studied in the photographs published in an 1896 booklet and in two museum collections that have been preserved intact since 1897. The early 1896 booklet entitled "Tiffany Favrile Glass" was the first publication concerning blown iridescent glass put out by the Tiffany Glass and Decorating Company. In a second edition, copyrighted in August 1896, an addendum gave the following statement:

It has been asked how Mr. Tiffany obtains his iridescent and lustre effects. The answer is by a careful study of the natural decay of glass, and by checking this process, by reversing the action in such a way as to arrive at the effects without disintegration. This will be better understood by reading the following words of Sir David Brewster, "There is perhaps no material body (glass) that ceases to exist with so much grace and beauty, when it surrenders itself to time and not to disease."

The quotation from the Scotch physicist went on to explain the chemistry of the decomposition of glass, but gave no hint about the method used by Tiffany to simulate the process with new glass.

The eight photographs that illustrated the 1896 booklet showed twelve examples of Tiffany glass (Ills. 31–38). It is not difficult to see, even from the black-and-white photographs, why this glass was then and still is highly prized by collectors. Its qualities are particularly apparent in the two vases intaglio-carved with leaves and flowers. Today it is also evident that all these forms are consistent with the style now generally known as Art Nouveau.

One of these items, the jar with the lid, can be seen in the Smithsonian Institution in Washington, D.C. Other examples of Tiffany blown glass acquired by the Smithsonian in 1896 were presented in *Rebel in Glass,* pages 166–169. Another group, also still available for study, was acquired by the Cincinnati Art Museum in 1897. This is of particular interest, since the museum has preserved the original bill of sale with the original numbers and prices (Ill. 39). It clearly demonstrates two facts: Tiffany's did sell cracked pieces at half price, and the ware was not cheap when it was new. The purchasing power of the dollar was much greater then than it is today—fifty dollars in 1900 was equivalent to over three hundred dollars now.

31–38. TIFFANY FAVRILE GLASS PHOTOGRAPHS PUBLISHED IN 1896.

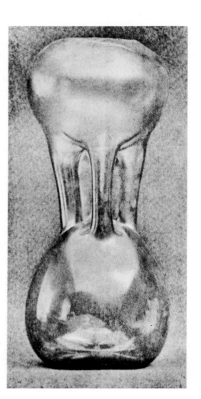

32

31

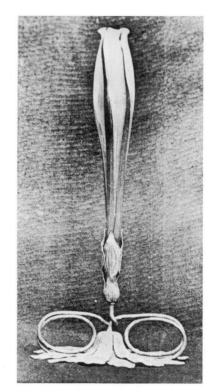

34

33

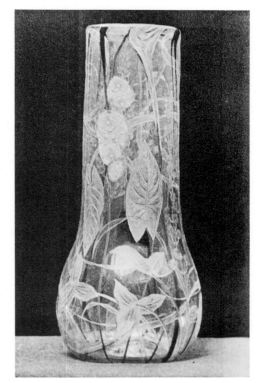

35

36

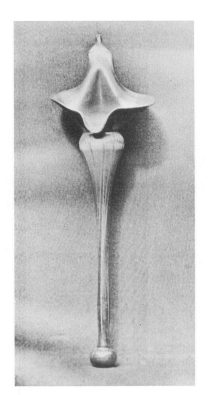

37

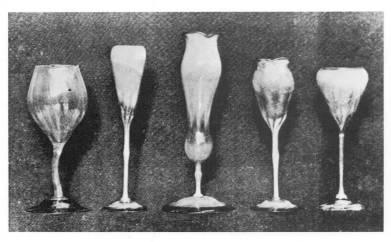

38

39. Bill of sale, July 1, 1897, of Tiffany glass to the Cincinnati Museum.

40–49. PHOTOGRAPHS (MADE IN 1970) OF TEN OF THE ITEMS LISTED
ON THE 1897 BILL OF SALE. *Courtesy of the Cincinnati Art Museum.*

	Accession #	*Tiffany #*	*Original Price (less 15%)*
40.		318	$15.00
41.	1897.120	X994,S404	18.00, Stand 3.00
42.	1897.125	4884 (cracked)	5.00
43.	1897.127	1163	15.00
44.	1897.128	1170	12.00
45.	1897.131	X1996	25.00
46.	1897.135	4373	50.00
47.	1897.136	X2971	50.00
48.	1897.137	5605	30.00
49.	1897.138	4882 (cracked)	7.50

40

41

42

43

44

45

46

47

48

49

Tiffany Furnaces was organized physically with sixteen pots grouped as eight arches, two "glory holes" in each arch. Some were used for lime glass, to make sheets for lamps and windows; others were for red-lead glass for blowing. For the entire thirty-five years of production only eight gaffers were employed. Each gaffer had a five-man shop, including a server, a gatherer, a decorator, and two helpers. The names of the gaffers were as follows:

1. Thomas Manderson, who created the first flower-form vases
2. George J. Cook, who developed the formula for Peacock glass. He left in 1909.
3. James H. Grady, of Sandwich, Massachusetts, who also produced Trevaise glass in his hometown
4. Arthur E. Saunders, whose specialty was aquamarine glass. He came in 1900 and left in 1918.
5. John Hollingsworth, who started as Manderson's server and replaced him as gaffer

50. Display of Tiffany Glass in the United States Pavilion at the Paris Exposition in 1900.

51. George ("Dutch") Gipson cleaning out one of the glass pots at Tiffany Furnaces.

52. Jimmy Stewart's shop at work in Tiffany Furnaces circa 1920.

6. Thomas Johnson, who later worked for Quezal Co.
7. Joseph Matthews
8. James A. Stewart, who became a gaffer only in 1918, but who had been employed in all other capacities in Corona since 1895.

Other important craftsmen employed in the Tiffany glass furnaces were Martin Bach, the first mixer, who resigned when he was accused of divulging the formulas, and later produced Quezal glass; and the two engravers, the first named Kreshner, who died in Corona and was replaced by Ernest Flogel.

At the peak of its production, Tiffany Furnaces turned out almost 30,000 items of blown glass each year, the bulk of which were blown shades for lamps that could be completed at the rate of four an hour in each shop. With five shops operating, a thousand such shades could be produced in one week.

Tiffany's glassmen were unionized and had absolutely no labor problems. In 1897 Tiffany's employees also organized a mutual aid association that provided many fringe benefits. Jimmy Stewart once told me, "There never was a better boss."

After a blown glass object was fully formed, it was annealed in a lehr or oven, where it remained for one week. It was then removed and placed on a table or shelf to wait for the finisher. There was no predetermined length of time that an object could be so stored. Some items remained without being finished or marked for several years.

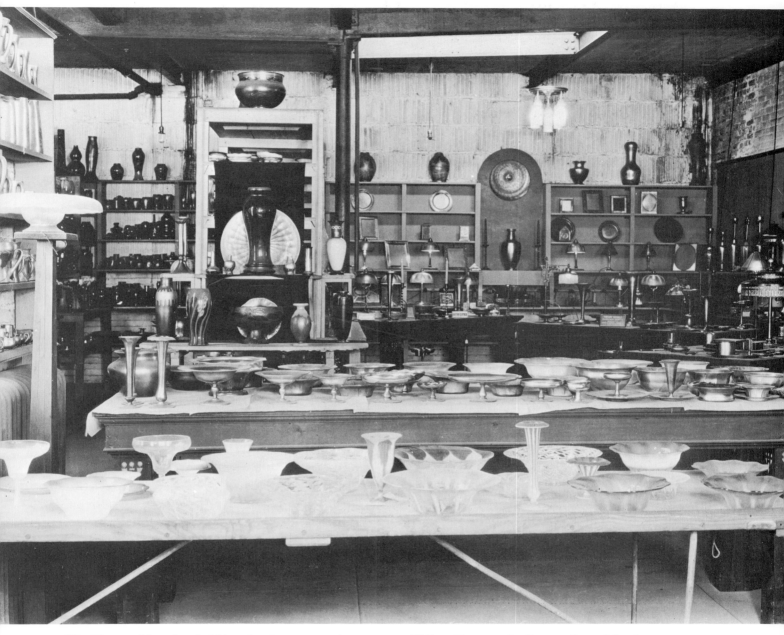

53. Glass waiting for finishing in the storage showroom at Tiffany Furnaces in Corona, Long Island.

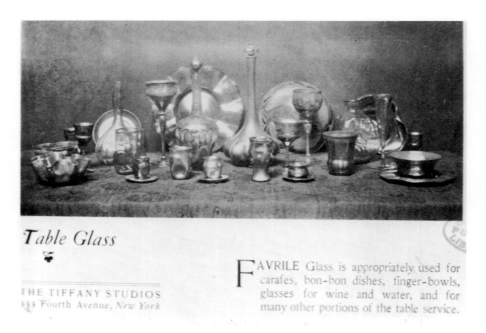

Table Glass

THE TIFFANY STUDIOS
Fourth Avenue, New York

FAVRILE Glass is appropriately used for carafes, bon-bon dishes, finger-bowls, glasses for wine and water, and for many other portions of the table service.

54. Glass tableware in Tiffany Studios in 1902.

In the finishing department the pontil mark was polished and the object cut or engraved, if desired; then it was signed, numbered, and registered for retail sale, and finally it was shipped out. If a vase was purchased by an employee or even a friend of an employee at the Corona plant, it was usually not signed or numbered. When, in 1928, the remaining stock of Tiffany Furnaces was placed on the market, most of the ware was not signed or registered. Thus, there is still a fair amount of unsigned Tiffany to be found. This can be recognized only by the quality of the glass, which is often unmistakable to a collector who has become familiar with well-documented examples.

The numbering and registering of Tiffany glass prior to 1919 was for purposes of retail sales alone. There were no wholesalers. Every item went out to distributors on consignment. That way, each piece could be readily identified. The system of numbering was as follows: During the first years of production, the numbers were in sequence from 1 to 9999, with the letter X indicating "experimental." Then, instead of going to five numbers, the prefix A was used. Hence, the ten-thousandth piece was registered and marked as A1, and thereafter so on through the alphabet. Most of the vases exhibited in Paris in 1900 were numbered with the prefix M or N. By 1906 it was necessary to switch from a prefix to a suffix, and they began again, with 1A. I have worked out a table of approximate corresponding numbers and years, but it should be used cautiously. It cannot be accurate except as to the terminal date before which an item was made. Also, there are an increasing number of forgeries with false numbers. The explanation of the numbering system was published in *Antiques* in a letter from Tiffany Furnaces that appeared under "Questions and Answers," number 329, page 478, December 1926.

TRADE-MARK.

No. 42,012.

REGISTERED FEB. 9, 1904.

TIFFANY FURNACES.
DECORATIVE GLASSWARE.
APPLICATION FILED MAY 29, 1903.

Witnesses:

Proprietor.

55. Trademark used for glass after 1902.

TIFFANY FAVRILE BLOWN GLASS

Registry Numbers by Years

1892–93	1–9999	1911	Suffix F
1894	Prefix A and B	1912	Suffix G
1895	Prefix C and D	1913	Suffix H
1896	Prefix E and F	1914	Suffix I
1897	Prefix G and H	1915	Suffix J *
1898	Prefix I and J *	1916	Suffix K
1899	Prefix K and L	1917	Suffix L
1900	Prefix M and N *	1918	Suffix M *
1901	Prefix O and P	1919	Suffix N
1902	Prefix Q and R	1920	Suffix O
1903	Prefix S and T	1921	Suffix P
1904	Prefix U and V *	1922	Suffix Q
1905	Prefix W and Y	1923	Suffix R
1906	Suffix A *	1924	Suffix S
1907	Suffix B	1925	Suffix T
1908	Suffix C	1926	Suffix U
1909	Suffix D	1927	Suffix V
1910	Suffix E	1928	Suffix W

---

* Dates confirmed by exhibition pieces.

Exceptions:

Prefix "S" also used for Blown Glass Shades and Globes

Prefix "X" means "Experimental"

Prefix "EX" means "For Exhibition"

Prefix small "o" means "Special Order" (the only number system to run over 10,000)

Suffix "A-COLL" means "For Louis C. Tiffany's Private Collection" (less than 250 so marked)

Prefix "P" designates "Pottery"; "BP" is for "Bronze Pottery"

Prefixes "EL," "EC," "SG" designate "Enamels"

The decrease in the number of unique, individually registered items after 1906 corresponds to an increase in the number of matched sets of tableware items that were not registered singly. A booklet issued in 1905 indicates the names given to some of the Tiffany tableware patterns. "Flemish" has applied glass thread; "Earl" is stretched glass;

"Royal" pattern has a twisted stem. The "Prince" and "Queen" patterns were made in the greatest quantity. These were often engraved with a grapevine design, and sometimes were made of blue glass. The blue is now more desirable and rarer, and so it is also more expensive. This 1905 booklet also illustrated glass shades, and showed that a completely different number system was used for shades.

The advanced collector, where price is no object, will look for the more complex and more unusual examples of Tiffany glass, but finding them seems to grow more and more difficult. The very fine examples of Tiffany—Lava, Cypriote, Agate, and Aquamarine glass similar to those illustrated in *Rebel in Glass*—are almost impossible to locate except when they appear in the important auctions in New York, Chicago, or London. At such a sale in October 1970, more than a dozen of the rarer Tiffany vases sold for over $1,000 each; one, an exhibition piece, brought $4,000.

56–67. THE TWELVE ILLUSTRATIONS THAT FOLLOW ARE PAGES FROM A TIFFANY BOOKLET PUBLISHED IN 1905.

TIFFANY FAVRILE GLASS

"FLEMISH" DESIGN

Light Shaded Gold, with Iridescent Lustre

This Suite of Glass comprises Liqueur, Claret, Sherry, Champagne and Decanter

TIFFANY FAVRILE GLASS

"VICTORIA"　　"EARL"　　"ASCOT"
"PRINCE"　　　　　　　"QUEEN"

FINGER BOWLS AND ICE PLATES

Light Shaded Gold, with Iridescent Lustre

TIFFANY FAVRILE GLASS

"ROYAL" DESIGN

Rich Golden Lustre

This Suite of Glass comprises Liqueur, Sherry, Claret, Hock and Champagne

58

TIFFANY FAVRILE GLASS

"PRINCESS"   "PRINCESS"   "MANHATTAN"
(Hock)   (Champagne)   (Champagne)

"DOMINION"   "PRINCE"   "ROYAL"   "SAVOY"
(Champagne)   (Champagne) (Champagne) (Champagne)

HOCK AND CHAMPAGNE GLASSES

Rich Golden Lustre

59

TIFFANY FAVRILE GLASS

F   H   E   C   G
A   I   B   D

COMPORTS, EPERGNES, BON BON DISHES, PLATES AND
PIN TRAYS

Light Shaded Gold, with Iridescent Lustre

A—"Queen" Comport, low . . . . 3 in.   4 in.   6 in. Dia.
B—"Queen" Comport, high . . . . 4 in.   6 in.   8 in. Dia.
C—"Colonial" Comport, low . . . 3 in.   4 in.   6 in.   8 in. Dia.
D—"Colonial" Comport, high . . . 4 in.   6 in.   8 in. Dia.
E—"Earl" Comport . . . . 4 in.   6 in.   8 in. Dia.
F—"Prince" Epergne . . . . . . 11 in.   14 in. high
G—"Iris" Epergne . . . . 11 in.   14 in. high
H—"Ascot" Plate . . . . 3 in.   3½ in.   4 in. Dia.
I —"Queen" Bon Bon Dish or Pin Tray 2½ in.   3 in.   4 in.   5 in. Dia.

60

TIFFANY FAVRILE GLASS

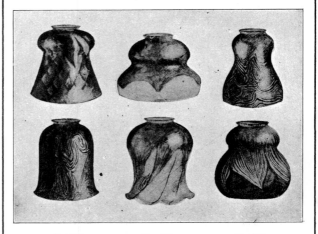

No. 178   No. 109   No. 111
No. 110   No. 134   No. 112

ELECTRIC LIGHT SHADES FOR 2¼ INCH FITTER

No. 178 4⅜ in. high 3¾ in. diameter 4¼ in. opening 2¼ in. fitter
No. 110 4½ in. "   3½ in.   "   4 in.   "   2¼ in. "
No. 109 4 in.   "   5¼ in.   "   4¼ in.   "   2¼ in. "
No. 134 5 in.   "   4⅜ in.   "   4¼ in.   "   2¼ in. "
No. 111 5 in.   "   4 in.   "   3½ in.   "   2¼ in. "
No. 112 4⅜ in. "   4¼ in.   "   2¼ in.   "   2¼ in. "

61

TIFFANY FAVRILE GLASS

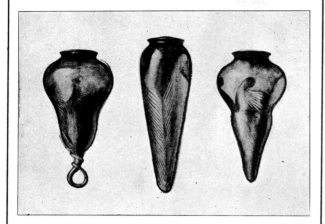

No. 137   No 128   No. 136

STALACTITES FOR ELECTRIC LIGHT

No. 137 12 in. high 5¾ in. diameter 3¼ in. fitter

No. 128 9 in. high 4½ in. diameter 3¼ in. fitter

15 in. high 5 in. diameter 3¼ in. fitter

No. 136 11¼ in. high 8¼ in. diameter 3¼ in. fitter

62

TIFFANY FAVRILE GLASS

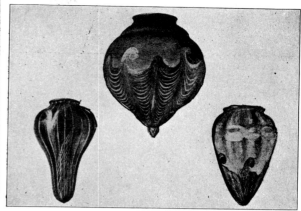

No 125   No. 127   No. 116

STALACTITES FOR ELECTRIC LIGHTING

No. 125 10½ in. high 5 in. diameter 3¼ in. fitter

No. 127 14 in. high 12 in diameter 5 in. fitter

No. 116 11 in. high 6 in. diameter 4½ in. fitter

63

TIFFANY FAVRILE GLASS

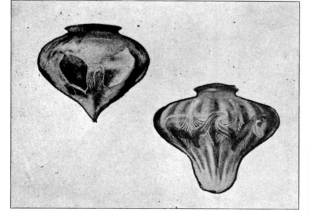

No. 185   No. 115

STALACTITES FOR ELECTRIC LIGHTING

No. 185 8¼ in. high 10½ in. diameter, for 5 in. fitter

No. 115 8½ in. high 10 in. diameter, for 4½ in. fitter

64

TIFFANY FAVRILE GLASS

"DAMASCENE" DESIGN

DOME SHADES

Green Opalescent, Gold Decoration, Lined with White or Ivory Opalescent, Gold Decoration

For Oil and Electric Light

7 in.   10 in.   12 in.   14 in.   Diameter

65

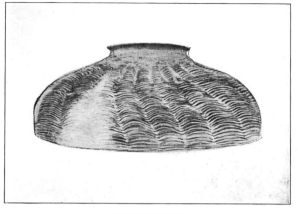

"WAVE" DESIGN

DOME SHADES

Green Opalescent, Gold Decoration, Lined with White or Ivory Opalescent, Gold Decoration

For Oil and Electric Light

7 in.   10 in.   12 in.   14 in. Diameter

"ETRUSCAN" DESIGN

DOME SHADES

Green Opalescent, Gold Decoration, Lined with White or Ivory Opalescent, Gold Decoration

For Oil and Electric Light

7 in.   10 in.   12 in.   14 in. Diameter

As major museums are adding these kinds of items to their collections, they are rapidly going off the market. The sketchbook of Jimmy Stewart, never before published, which concludes the next chapter (Chapter 6), gives a fresh look at the variety of shapes and decorations of Tiffany vases during the peak years of their production. It also provides the names of the gaffers, thus helping to distinguish the particular contributions of each of these craftsmen.

The late phase, from 1918 to 1928, is frequently called the Nash period of Tiffany Furnaces. At this time the supervision of glassmaking was left to A. Douglas Nash, the son of Arthur J. Nash, who retired from active participation in 1918.

Arthur Nash had three sons—Douglas, Leslie, and Bredt. As young men all three worked for their father at Tiffany's, but they did not get along. Bredt moved to Connecticut, and Leslie founded his own factory in Woodside, New York, leaving A. Douglas Nash to manage Tiffany Furnaces. Jimmy Stewart stayed on as gaffer.

During the twenties the line of Tiffany glass changed, but not enough to keep up with the trend of the times. The most notable difference in the glass of the last decade of Tiffany Furnaces is in the colors. Pastel colors with a thin iridescence were featured instead of the rich golds, blues, and dark greens of the Art Nouveau. The new pale colors—yellows, light blues, pinks, and light greens—went over well at first but were not commercially successful over the years.

The Tiffany name, signatures, marks, and numbers continued without interruption in this late period. It was not until after 1928 that Tiffany-type glass was produced at Tiffany Furnaces and signed either ADNA or NASH. This, however, is one Tiffany-type glass that cannot be distinguished from the real thing, since it too was made by the same Jimmy Stewart. The A. Douglas Nash Company continued to run what had been the Tiffany Furnaces until 1931. In that year the fires were permanently extinguished.

Finally, a word of advice: Collect glass, not signatures. It is virtually impossible to be sure the signature on a piece of Tiffany glass is authentic. The name or initials were cut or etched into the glass by workmen, and they vary in size and style according to who did the job. Usually smaller objects have only the initials, whereas others have a full name. The initials L. C. T. appear as block letters more often than in script, but both are valid. There is a manuscript signature, Louis C. Tiffany, in his own handwriting style, that appears on some of the more important examples. But again, it is more valuable to know the glass than to know the signatures. Until the collector is sure that he can recognize a piece of Tiffany glass, signed or unsigned, it is advisable that he deal with only the most reliable sources. With experience and knowledge comes recognition of the quality of the glass, which must be evident. No other glass, European or American, ever achieved the same kind of harmony of material, body shape, and decoration that is the true hallmark of Tiffany glass.

If a piece of unsigned Tiffany glass has a forged signature, the forgery is often virtually impossible to detect. However, the registry number often added by the forger is almost always totally invalid. Sometimes it is possible to recognize a recently added signature by its placement on the glass. I once bought some early Tiffany bowls with forged L. C. T.'s scratched crudely on the pontil marks on the bottom. I had the scratched initials removed by a man who could polish the glass without damaging it, thus restoring the bowls to their original condition as unsigned Tiffany. Forged Tiffany signatures have also appeared on Steuben Aurene glass, Quezal, Durand, Webb bronze, and Loetz glass. All such pieces are worth less with forged signatures than they would have been if left unsigned, for an expert to identify. Unfortunately, many fine examples of iridescent art glass have been spoiled by the addition of fake signatures that cannot be removed.

SIX

AN INTERVIEW WITH JIMMY STEWART, TIFFANY GAFFER

(Recorded April 6, 1966)

R.K.—This recording is being made in the home of Mr. James A. Stewart, who worked for Tiffany Furnaces from February 11, 1895, until they closed shop in 1928. I am going to ask Mr. Stewart a few questions, and I am going to begin by asking him to tell us about the beginning of his career when he first went to work at the furnaces. Mr. Stewart, please . . .

J.S.—When I started at the Tiffany Furnaces they had one cathedral glass or window glass shop and one blowing shop. Now, the gaffer on the blowing shop was Tom Manderson from Gillinder Bros.[1] in

---

[1] In 1861 The Franklin Flint Glass Works was established in Philadelphia by William T. Gillinder. Six years later the name was changed to Gillinder and Sons and later became Gillinder Brothers. At the Philadelphia Centennial of 1876 they exhibited both blown and pressed glass and introduced cameo glass in 1880. In 1912 the Gillinder Brothers moved to Port Jervis, N.Y. McKearin, *American Glass,* page 610.

Philadelphia. His blower or second man in the shop was John Hollingsworth, who was his server; his son, Bill Manderson, was the decorator; the gatherer was George Parker. That made up the shop, with two boys. One was the dip boy and the other was the taking-in boy. I was the taking-in boy. Marty Bach was the mixer who made up the glass.

R.K.—Would you please tell me, Mr. Stewart, about what you learned of Tiffany Furnaces prior to the time that you came to work there.

J.S.—In 1892 there had been a hand laundry in this building that we occupied later on. In 1893 the place was burned down. In fact there was one casualty in there, the night man—he never came back. The bosses at that time were the Nash family. There was only one Nash there when I went in—that was Mr. Nash himself, the elderly gentleman.[2] Later on, his son Douglas came in and then his son Leslie came in. They were the only real bosses in there. The gaffer was the boss of the gang that he worked; while he worked, he was the head of the shop. He went through all of the different degrees that we went through. Before I was a gaffer, I had been a dip boy and then I was promoted to a gatherer. I was promoted from the window glass or cathedral glass shop to a blowing shop because I figured there was no more for me to learn in the cathedral shop, so I wanted to go over to the hot metal department, which I did. I became a gatherer, then I became a decorator, naturally; then I became a blower at one of the shops. In 1918 there was a rumor that they were going to put on another shop.[3] I went down to the office and had a chat with the big boss and told him I would like to have that job in case it did materialize. And he says, "All right, Jimmy, if we put on a new shop you're going to be the gaffer," and thank God I was because I loved my work. Yeah, I surely did. There wasn't anything they asked me to do in that factory that I didn't do. I had my own time to do it—if it was a press or window glass machine or decorating or gathering, I was, I would say, an all-around man.

---

[2] Arthur J. Nash, born 1849, had been a manager of the Webb Glasshouse and came from the Stourbridge district of England in 1891 or 1892. According to James Stewart he came to the United States as a sales representative for English glass. The first name that he proposed for Tiffany Furnaces was the Stourbridge Glass Works of Corona and the first blown products were called Corona glass. It was A. J. Nash who suggested the name "Fabrile," later "Favrile," as the trademark for Tiffany glass.

[3] Stewart's shop in 1918 was the fifth blowing shop at Tiffany Furnaces at the time. On other occasions James Stewart has told me about the gaffers in charge of the other shops.

R.K.—Now please explain some of the problems of obtaining the iridescent colors that are the special feature of Tiffany glass.

J.S.—The Tiffany iridescent colors were first applied to the window glass, lime glass, but at first they had trouble with the blowing glass, which is red-lead glass. I was there the day that we hit the colors, that we made the first vase of Tiffany iridescent glass. That was in 1895. He, Mr. Tiffany himself, was down in his office with Mr. Nash and his chemist, and I am positive I was sent down to the office to bring Mr. Tiffany up to show him this new vase that he never saw before. When he came up he was so delighted—I can see him prancing around and dancing around there yet, and pulling his belt up and so on and so forth, yeah. So from that day on until they closed down, Tiffany's colors were all over the United States and all over the world. Every big museum in Europe and every large museum that I can think of had an exhibit of Tiffany. These colors that we produced were iridescent, tinted chemically. But we had to prepare a vase before we applied the chemicals to produce those colors. Now, if you applied too much in preparing them for their colors, you deaden the color. If you didn't get it enough, if you were very skimpy, your colors didn't stand out at all. So we had to prepare our glass before we applied the chemicals, and Dr. McIlhenny [4] was about the fourth or fifth chemist they had there before he produced the chemicals that produced these Tiffany colors.

R.K.—How about the members of the Nash family? Were they glass-blowers and, if not, what did they do in the factory?

J.S.—I recall when I went to work in that factory Mr. Nash was the boss—under Mr. Tiffany, of course—and I always understood that Mr. Tiffany was the man who accepted or rejected a shape. Now when he'd go to Florida or go to Europe, Mr. Nash would come out —and even when Mr. Tiffany was in New York—Mr. Nash had a big blackboard in back of every gaffer, and when a new shape was coming into existence, he would draw that shape with a piece of chalk on that blackboard. [5] He would shade it with his thumb, with his finger—he would shade it, the light and the dark part. Then we would take our calipers and we'd set our calipers to that bowl or vase or dish, or whatever it may be, and we'd get enough glass out to

---

[4] Dr. Parker McIlhenny remained as Tiffany's chemist for more than twenty years.

[5] This accounts for the fact that no drawings have survived of Tiffany vases. James Stewart did keep a sketchbook of his own with some of the more interesting Tiffany shapes that are to be found. The sketches are reproduced following this interview.

make that size bowl or vase or whatever. Then the decorator would decorate it and take it to the server, and the server would blow it, and the blower would send it over to the gaffer, and the gaffer would prepare it for its colors—put the finishing touches on the finishing of it and put the colors on. That was my job, for ten years. I liked my work—in fact, I loved it, yeah, I did. Every piece was a beautiful thing. Every piece was something out of this world.

Now as I knew Mr. Nash—A.J., that was the elderly gentleman, the father of the three or four boys—I never knew him in all my experience in the shop that he ever blew a piece of glass, never. I used to see him go over to the furnace and take a—what they call a pontil, and he would dip it into the glass and take a little bit out, and he didn't know enough to turn the pontil around to keep it in balance, and it would drip down to the floor—naturally the brick floor was in there. I didn't ever know any of the Nashes ever blowing anything, none of them. Absolutely none. As one of them said to me one time, "I can go into the shop and do a little carpenter work and a little tinsmithing work and like that, but I tried your glass and I couldn't do a God-blessed thing with it." So after all, they were no glassblowers.[6] They was manager; they knew an article when they saw it, and they knew how to sketch out an article for you—yeah, and then when we had it all finished, it was beautiful, it surely was beautiful. That's the only thing I can term it as, *beautiful.* I would like to say that Mr. A. J. Nash was one of the finest bosses that I ever heard of, never mind worked for. I worked for a couple of bosses in the summertime and like that, but there was none of them compared with Mr. Nash.

Now his son, Douglas, he took care of the office. He was down the office all the time. He was vice-president of the company and secretary, and Leslie was the production manager. I want to say that Leslie was a fine boss—he was a fine boss, yes. When he come to you, when he was going to try something, he wouldn't come bulldozing like the majority of bosses do, that I saw and worked for. He'd just say, "Well, Jimmy, we're gonna try something new." *We* are gonna try, not *I.*

R.K.—Now, Mr. Stewart, you've told me that you were the person who made all the tiles, all the scarab beetles, all the pressed glass

---

[6] In *Louis C. Tiffany, Rebel in Glass,* I characterized A. J. Nash as a "wizard of the blow-pipe." According to James Stewart this was an error; it has been corrected in the second edition by the substitution of the name of Thomas Manderson.

that was ever made in the shop. Do you want to tell us about what kind of work that was?

J.S.—Now in regard to the tiles, we made all sorts of tiles. Long ones, narrow ones, wide ones, turtlebacks, scarab bugs, and those glass jewels on lampshades we called mummy beads, imitating beads that was taken off the mummies on the island of Cyprus in the catacombs there. Some of them they used in Tiffany's Furnaces and some of them were used when they make a tile mantelpiece . . . they had the scarab bugs and they had the mummy beads and they had them inserted all here and there and they were beautiful, too.[7]

My boss come through this particular lunchtime and he said, "Jimmy, how would you like to press a couple of turtlebacks?" and I said, "I don't know, I don't know anything about them." "Oh, yes, you do now, don't tell me that." So, all right. I made three or four turtlebacks and put them in the tempering lehr. First thing you know the boss is out with the turtlebacks and he wants three hundred of them made. That's when I was making cathedral glass [between 1898 and 1900] and I did that [all pressing] up until the time they closed down.[8]

Every now and then I put in a half a day overtime. We wasn't supposed to have overtime, glassmakers, not in America or Canada. If they had enough work for a man to go overtime, they'd hire some other fellow who wasn't working at all. That's how they kept everybody pleased. But if it was in a plant like ours . . . they couldn't get an outside man to come in and do the press work; he didn't know about producing the colors and the like of that. So I used to put in an extra, what we called a move—four hours was a move, two moves was a day's work—eight hours. And I used to get the boys that worked with me to work with me—one was a gatherer and they'd alternate, they'd work a half an hour and rest a half an hour. Because of the intense heat in that factory, sometimes you had to put your head out the window to get some fresh air in your lungs, or go over and put both arms to your elbows into half a barrel of water to cool the blood off in your wrist, your pulse. But I was in

---

[7] There were three presses at Tiffany Furnaces, as explained in Chapter 3. (See Ill. 6.) At the peak of his career, Stewart could turn out 200 turtleback tiles in an hour. He was unable to estimate how many he produced altogether. None of the other workers were allowed to operate the presses. Turtleback tiles were pressed individually on the medium-sized press.

[8] Turtleback tiles are irregularly shaped glass of gold, blue, or green iridescent colors about six inches long by 5 inches wide. They were mostly used in lamps and lighting fixtures.

there for thirty-three years and I guess I liked it. If I didn't I wouldn't have stayed in there. Half of the boys in Corona worked in there, but they couldn't see any future. There was no other glasshouse like it, so if somebody didn't die, there was never an opening for promotion until you got to be a gaffer yourself. I was the only one of the hundreds of boys in our town of Corona—working in that factory there—I was the only boy that made the grade. Thank God I did.

R.K.—Earlier you mentioned Marty Bach as the mixer in 1895. Is that the same Martin Bach, Sr., who made Quezal glass?

J.S.—That's right. He had a disagreement with the boss in there, and he made up his mind he was going to leave. He had the idea he was going to make Tiffany kind of glass, but there was no mechanic on the outside that could produce the glass that he wanted, the imitation of the Tiffany. So he took a job as a conductor on the BMT, the Brooklyn trolley cars that run to North Beach, from Maspeth. There was a chap who had some difficulty in the shop named Tom Johnson. He was working as a gaffer in there for a few months on trial before he had this little disturbance. And when the other gaffer came back they had a real upset, so Mr. Nash let Johnson out and they kept the other gaffer. That just fitted right in Marty Bach's book—that's just what he wanted. He got in touch with Johnson, who opened a little stationery store in Long Island City, him and his wife, and that's what he was doing—he wasn't working at the glass business. So Bach got in touch with him and that's just what Bach wanted—he needed a man out of Tiffany's, and he went out and got that discarded fellow from Tiffany's and he started the Quezal Art Glass Company.[9]

A little glass factory down there wasn't doing much—there was two ladies, two sisters, running it, the Donnerhoff sisters, and he got in touch with them, he rented a pot, one of the girls' glass pots, and proved that he could produce the Tiffany glass.[10] That was his stock, when he hired the pot and put the luster glass in the pot and melted it up and it was perfect, just what he wanted. That opened up his career for him, and I guess he was in business for twenty or twenty-five years, until he passed out and his son took it over, and his son didn't do so well. He left there and he went to Vineland,

---

[9] Johnson (there were two Johnsons who were not related to each other) did not stay with Bach for long. Later he went to Somerville, Mass., where he made Kew Blas glass for William S. Blake at the Union Glass Company.

[10] Quezal glass was first made in 1902 as a Tiffany-type iridescent art glass.

New Jersey—there was a French manufacturer there.[11] Bach was a Frenchman—Alsace-Lorraine, that's where he come from. He wanted me to go with him when he first left Tiffany, and I wouldn't leave Tiffany. But at any rate he was there for twenty or twenty-five years, down in Maspeth. And the son who went to Vineland, New Jersey, was only there a short time, but Vineland was making the iridescent glass and it was young Bach who was making it, so that's all I know about that plant.

R.K.—Could you tell us now, Mr. Stewart, how a Tiffany vase was made? Let us begin with the most elaborate type, the kind known as aquamarine glass using a paperweight technique.

J.S.—I'll try and explain how this glass was made up.[12] When you would look at it, its color was inside; its outside was a flint color, transparent, you could look through it. Now, we decorated on the outside, and we would go back in the furnace again and put another layer of clear glass over that. Now the way they decorate that would be six or eight or ten dots of green glass on the first gather that we gather out. We would round that up with the heat in the glory hole, would round it all up, and we'd flatten them out and then we'd make a leaf with that little green dot. We'd run stems all over it. You'd put the hot threads of glass on the pontil and the hot vase in the furnace at 3300° Fahrenheit, and as soon as you put it in there, the heat would blow the stems, blow stems all over it, and it would just stick out like a vine and the little green leaves.[13]

Previous to that we would make cane, and the cane would be five petals of white, we'll say, a little dot of yellow; we'd put dark yellow around that little white dot and put it in a 16-rib blower, just shove it down in like 16 little beads; then we'd go back to the furnace and gather out maybe 10 or 12 pounds, and we'd draw that from you to me or from me to you, with the boy. We would take the boy, he would go away from you, he would pull that end; I would go away from the boy and I would pull my end. Then we'd pull down the thread to about the size of a lead pencil. We'd let that solidify, and we would break it off in four- or six-feet lengths. Then

---

[11] Martin Bach, Sr., was born April 21, 1865, in Rahling, near Sarreguemines (Moselle) and began work in the St. Louis glasshouse. He died in 1921. In 1924 his son, Martin Bach, Jr., went to work for the Durand Art Glass Co. in Vineland, N.J., according to Samuel Farber, "Durand Glass," *The Antiques Journal,* May 1961, pp. 8–12.

[12] This style today is generally called paperweight because the use of canes is similar to that which is traditional in the making of weights (millefiori technique).

[13] This is an example of the controlled accident that gave to many Tiffany vases their very modern look.

the cutters down the cutting shop would take that with a pair of pinchers they had, and they would slice that as thin as they could slice it. And the petals wouldn't be all the same size, naturally, because the piece wouldn't—you couldn't cut it like you would with a knife. Then we would place that center wherever we wanted. We cut five different cuts like that and opened those, pushed those white petals back, and right in the center we'd drop that little piece of cane that had a center in it, you know, like the center of a flower that has maybe a yellow center where there is six or seven little yellow dots or maybe brown or red. It all depends on what kind of cane we used—we used to make that all in there.

Then when we'd get the vase all decorated, we'd go back over to the furnace and put it down into the molten glass and put a layer on that. Now when the vase was finished, the last thing we do, we go over with the empty iron to the prepared batch, and gather a little iridescent glass, just a little tiny dip on the end of the blow-pipe, and that would be the lining when the vase was finished. That was the only glass that would take the colors, that lining, so we'd put the chemicals in the vase and move it around, and that would get us the iridescent color. When you look at it, it looked as if the decoration was under the water. Underwater glass, that's what we term it as.

R.K.—What were some of the other ways to decorate vases, and about how long did it take to make a vase?

J.S.—Oh, we had so many ways of decorating vases. There were never two days alike in the Tiffany's Furnaces, never. One day you got a shape you're working on that you make fourteen an hour; the next day you're working on a different shape, and you make maybe eight an hour or six an hour. You never, never put a number of how many you can do in an hour.[14] Some days your glass is good and some days your glass is not good. You get a furnace that is only half heated and you've got a thousand little bubbles in there. Every one of those bubbles is an arrested bubble—it's an arrested air bubble, and that air bubble is like a fellow in a prison that's trying to get out; the air's trying to get out of that little bubble.

You know, this glass is a queer substance. It does everything only what you want it to do, so you have to be the boss and make it do

---

[14] These figures of six to fourteen an hour refer to the making of matched items of tableware all of the same color. Vases always took longer; and the more different colors used, the more time they required. A blown dome-shaped lampshade took about twenty-five minutes for a shop to complete.

what you want it to do to get the shape. Now when I start to blow a vase, when I was in the blowing department, if I stopped at a certain time on that vase that I'm gonna make, putting [it] into the shape that I want it, I could stop fifty different times and have fifty different vases. You had to make it do what you want it to do. My work and my lifetime was production, not talk. Some people can talk all day and love it, but I can't. I'm a worker, yeah. We can always say decorators can get it prepared for their colors in about—maybe from the time the gatherer got it out till it was finished would be—maybe fifteen minutes, maybe twenty minutes. We made vases, not I, but one of the shops made vases there, I recall—they would make one in an hour, one complete vase in an hour—that would take almost fifteen minutes for the gatherer to get it out, another fifteen minutes for the blower to blow it, and another maybe a half hour for the gaffer to finish it. They made four in an afternoon, four in four hours.

R.K.—What kind of furnaces were used, and how did they work?

J.S.—Now the furnaces we worked at were running at 2800° Fahrenheit to 3000° Fahrenheit, and they were operated with crude oil and steam. Now to put the steam in there took all the smoke out of the oil, the crude oil that we used, and they would sometimes run those up to almost 4000° Fahrenheit. Every shop had three glory holes—one for the gaffer and two big ones for the gatherer, the blower, and the decorator. Six men worked to supply the gaffer, and it was up to him to finish the piece and prepare it for the colors. The gaffer had an individual glory hole of his own, so there were two big ones that three or four shops could work at at the same time. It was a sixteen-pot furnace, eight arches with two pots in each arch. Some of these were for lime window glass and some for red-lead blowing glass. These ran for seventeen years without the fires ever going out.

R.K.—What kind of raw materials were used for making the glass, and what kind of pots was it made in?

J.S.—In the summertime when we would be working in the glasshouse, we would take the broken pots and break them all up into small pieces, about as big as your hand, your fist, and in the bottom of those pots, specially the little monkey pots that hold about three hundred pounds, we'd find melted silver. I remember A.J. came through one time and he says, "Jimmy, did you hit a gold mine?" and I said, "Well, I hit a silver vein, I know that." "That's the boy," he said, "knock 'em out." We'd take it to New York, to one of these places downtown, and they'd give us thirty-five cents an ounce, forty cents an ounce—and you know, if you had a tomato can full of that silver metal, you had a nice vacation, and that's what we used to do in the summertime. A lot of the boys there would all work on the broken pots. Some pots you wouldn't get nothing in at all, absolutely. Others, the bottom was covered with silver—yeah, melted silver in all the little depressions down in the bottom of the pot.

Those pots were made in a layer of clay. They put a base down first, the bottom of the pot, and then on top of that they would put these rolls of clay, one roll on top of the other, and they'd smooth that all off until it was as smooth as glass on the outside and as smooth as glass on the inside. And it had a hood on it like a hog with its head off, you know, just its neck and a shoulder—that's the opening—and we used to throw the metal in there.

The metal was manufactured white sand, which originally was a silica rock. They'd grind that until they had it back into sand again. Pressure somewhere in the world had solidified that into a rock form. Now they would grind that up, as I say, in a machine until it was just a powder, and it was whiter than a white shirt. There's five different whites, I know that. But this was a white that was whiter than snow. That was that ground silica rock. Now you used so many hundred pounds of silica rock, so many hundred pounds of red lead, so many ounces of borax, so many ounces of potash, so many ounces of—about eight or ten different ingredients, I don't know them all, I can't say them all off. But I know what it takes to make a pot of glass.

R.K.—When a vase was finished, how was it annealed?

J.S.—When we'd make and finish the vase or bowl or glass, whatever it may be we were doing, we had to put that into a—what we called a lehr; it was a tempering lehr that was operated from 700° Fahrenheit to maybe about, say 800° or 825° Fahrenheit, to keep the glass from flying apart. Now we put that—all day · Monday's work— would be in about two or three iron pans that hooked onto each other. They were all separate but they were all hooked together out on the front, where we used to put the glass in to temper it. Human hands wouldn't touch that glass for one full week. The following Sunday that glass would start to come out down the end of 85 feet, down in the building, way down, and they would empty that lehr out, take all the glass out, take it in the inspection rooms. It would be inspected, and taken in the cutting shop where the cutters would take all the rough edges and all the buffing off and polish it, polish it up. Never on the luster glass because if they did that, they'd take the color all off, but just parts that wasn't colored with Tiffany color. They'd put the wheel on that and take all the rough edges off it. The bottom of the vase was just as smooth as what the inside was.[15] So it would take a full week from the time the article was made until human hands could touch it.

And another thing—the Tiffany people, they owned all the production of that factory until the time it was sold, and when you'd buy a vase—I don't care where you'd buy it, in San Francisco or Florida or New Jersey or where—you bought it from Tiffany because he owned it. The people who had it in their stores were only consignees; they got a percentage, I guess, for selling it. And three months they'd have it in Florida, and if they didn't dispose of it, they'd bring it back to our factory. Our factory would reship it to Philadelphia, we'll say, and it was there for three months. Then it would go to Chicago, Marshall Field, and they had it for three months, and if they didn't sell it, after nine months it had been shipped out three different times, they would break it up in a barrel.[16] Couldn't find no seconds in Tiffany—everything was perfect. That's the reason they had the cutters and engravers there; they'd take a lot of defects, cut them out altogether, take it off the piece altogether, redeem it, and make it a first-class piece. Every piece that went out of Tiffany's was first-class, and if it wasn't they'd break it up.

R.K.—One last question, Mr. Stewart, and this is for the collectors: Is every piece of blown Tiffany glass marked in some way?

J.S.—While we were working in there, there were some pieces that never got to the engravers and finishers, so they were never marked. You go to the one who the boss told you to go to when you wanted to get a piece, and if he'd forget to give you a receipt for your money—well, it was just too bad. Well, I got about four or five pieces that no one signed, unsigned by him, he never had them take it to the engravers, I never got a receipt for my money, so I figured

---

[15] There was almost no cut glass in the usual sense made by Tiffany, but the cutters and engravers did carve some items in either cameo or intaglio decorations.

[16] Only those items made with fewer than three colors were destroyed if they were not sold in nine months.

I may as well steal the stuff as pay $5 or $10 or $15 for a piece and I got no receipt to show that I'd paid it. He was a bottle baby—the fellow couldn't help it; he had to have that nourishment or he couldn't work, I guess. So after all, I stopped it altogether; I never stole anything. I'd go to New York and pay whatever they asked me.

Also, there are many pieces out today to people that have no mark—they're not marked. They were made in our factory but they were never recognized as Tiffany, never. When he passed out, he left all that unmarked and marked production to a man named Briggs, who run the Tiffany Studios downtown at Twenty-third Street for eight years through the Depression.[17] They were never signed by L.C.T., never, because they were to be redeemed in some way. Either the cutters or the engravers would engrave them and redeem them, make them a first-class piece. But after he passed out, Briggs took over six hundred and some odd thousand dollars' worth of stock Mr. Tiffany left Mr. Briggs. Now what he left the Foundation, I will never tell you because I never heard, to be honest about it. I never heard what he left the Foundation, but I know he left Mr. Briggs almost three-quarters of a million dollars' worth of stock that he had there. He didn't leave us anything—only his name, that's all. We worked on the Tiffany glass, yeah, that's all.

R.K.—Thank you, Mr. Stewart.

J.S.—Just one thing more. You say in your book that Mr. Tiffany wanted everybody to have his glassware.[18] Tiffany glass was never made for the poorer class of people, never. Mr. Tiffany did not want the poor people to have any of his glassware. It had to be the Goulds, the Sages, the Vanderbilts. Jay Gould's house, Seventy-fifth Street and Fifth Avenue, it was loaded with Tiffany, but his daughter disposed of the glassware.

R.K.—Thank you again, Mr. Stewart, and I will do what I can to set the record straight.

* * *

[17] Production at Tiffany Furnaces ended in 1928. Louis C. Tiffany died in 1933. Joseph Briggs died in 1938. During that decade much of the unsigned stock of glass was distributed, although some of it ended up in warehouses where it was stored until recently.

[18] In *Louis C. Tiffany, Rebel in Glass* I indicate that he "wanted to provide good art for American homes, to offer objects of quality for the widest possible audience." It was to this that James Stewart made an objection, and I realize now how it could be misunderstood. I did, however, in the book make it perfectly clear that Tiffany glass was always expensive and could be purchased only by those who could afford luxury items in glass.

The sketchbook of the late James A. (Jimmy) Stewart is the last source yet to come to light for an overall survey of Tiffany blown glass from 1893 until 1928. His sketches were stored away in 1945 and not again shown to anyone until a few months before Stewart's death in 1967. As they could not have been altered in any way during that period of more than twenty years, they must be regarded as entirely reliable. It should be noted that there is a ten-year gap, with no items dated between 1908 and 1918, the year that Stewart was promoted to gaffer at Tiffany Furnaces. All the sketches from that time on are of glass made by Stewart himself.

It was usual for gaffers at Tiffany's to keep notebooks with sketches. Such a notebook by George Joseph Cook (see Stewart's third sketch—Ill. 70), recently sold at auction at Parke-Bernet Galleries, was described in their catalogue as follows: "It contains about 85 glass batch recipes and descriptions of decorative surface treatments as well as about 70

SKETCHES BY JAMES A. STEWART

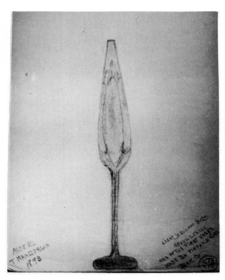

68. Made by T. Manderson 1893. Light yellow body, green leaves. One of the first vases made by Tiffany Glass and Decorating Co.

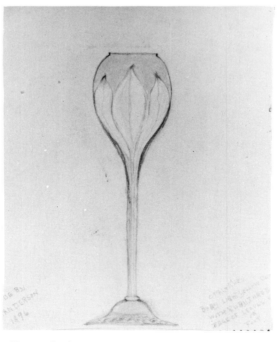

69. Made by T. Manderson 1896. Opal and ruby body, light yellow cup with ruby thread on edge of leaves, same on foot.

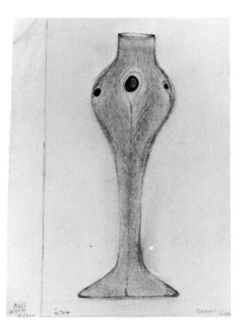

70. Peacock Vase 1899. Made by G Cook, #0.7250.

large and small outline drawings, mostly vase-like, characteristic of Tiffany production at this time, several with color suggestions." Cook resigned from Tiffany Furnaces in 1908. Another similar notebook kept by Arthur E. Saunders is also still in existence.

Stewart's sketchbook indicates that there was very little change in the style of shapes and decoration during the thirty-five years of production of Tiffany vases. His and the other notebooks also prove it is purely a myth that the Tiffany formulas were destroyed. Nevertheless, Tiffany glass cannot be reproduced. All the men who made it have died, and the conditions in which it was produced cannot be re-created. Tiffany vases will always remain the finest examples of the golden era of American art glass.

The captions on the illustrations taken from Stewart's sketchbook are actually the notes he himself put on the drawings.

71. Made by J. Grady 1902. Ruby body and cover, dark brown threading for deck[oration].

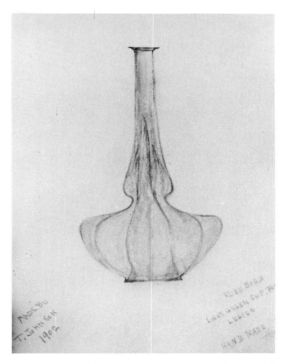

72. Made by T. Johnson 1902. Ruby body, light green cup for leaves. Hand made.

74. Made by E. Sa[u]nders 1905. Light orange body, light green cup for leaves, ruby and brown for dec[oration].

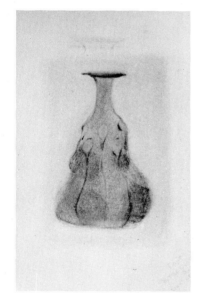

73. Made by J. Hollingworth 1904. Egyptian bottle, light brown body, light gray tear drops.

75. Made by E. Sa[u]nders 1906. Orange body, dark green cup for leaves, brown thread for decoration.

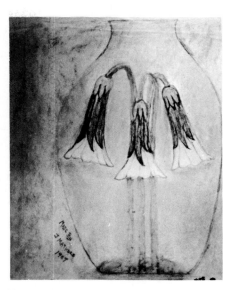

77. Made by J. Matthews 1907.

76. Made by E. Sa[u]nders 1907. Opal body, light green cup, green and orange decoration, dark green foot and lip.

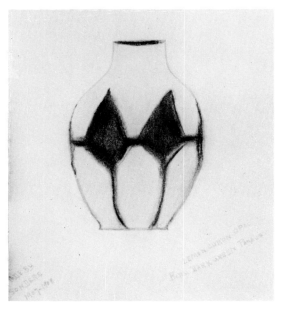

78. Made by E. Sa[u]nders 1907–08. Lemon cup on opal body, dark green panels.

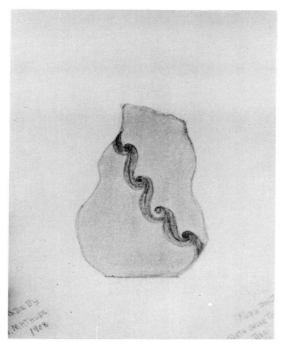

79. Made by J. Matthews 1908. Ruby body, slate color threading dec[oration].

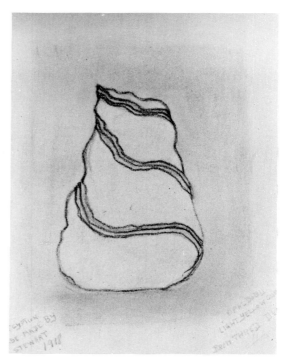

80. Egyptian vase made by J. Stewart 1918. Opal body, light yellow cup, brown thread decoration.

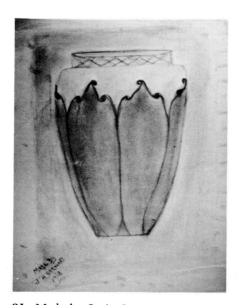

81. Made by J. A. Stewart 1918.

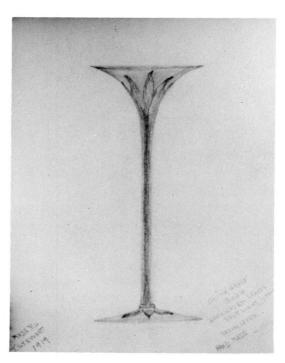

82. Made by J. Stewart 1919. Olive green body, dark green leaves, foot light yellow, green leves [*sic*] hand made.

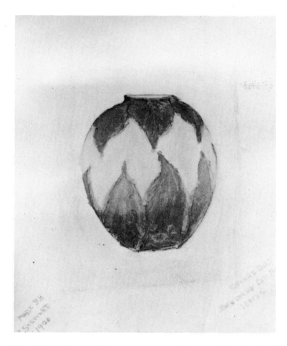

83. Made by J. Stewart 1920. Orange body, dark green cup for leaves.

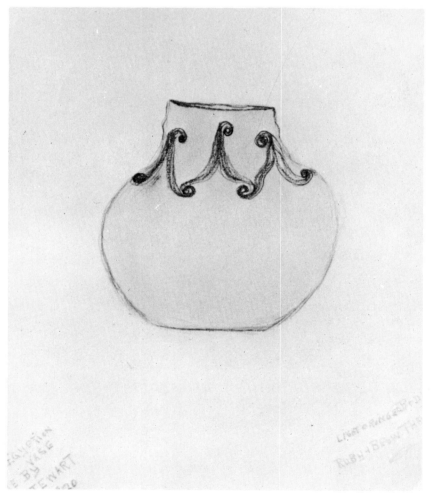

84. Egyptian vase made by J. Stewart 1920. Light orange body, ruby and brown threading.

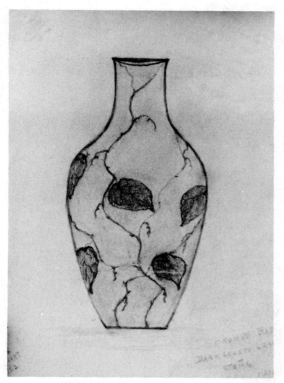

85. Made by J. Stewart 1922. Orange body, dark green leaves and stems. Handmade.

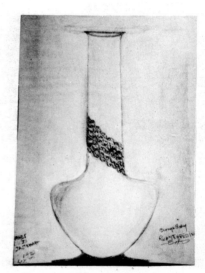

87. Made by J. A. Stewart 1923. Orange body, ruby threading.

86. Made by J. Stewart 1923. Flint body, green leaves, pink flowers.

88. Made by J. Stewart 1923. Ruby body, bluish green cup, brown ring on edge for leaves.

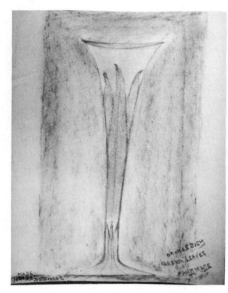

89. Made 1924 by J. Stewart. Orange body, green leaves, hand made.

90. Made by J. Stewart. Opal body, green stem and leaves, engraved flower, 1923.

91. Made by J. Stewart 1925. Light yellow body, green and orange leaves.

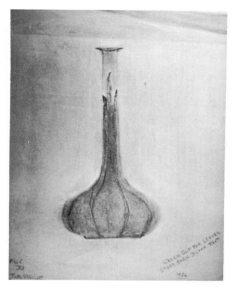

92. Made by J. A. Stewart. Green cup for leaves, orange body, black foot, 1926.

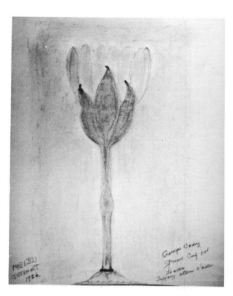

93. Made by J. Stewart 1926. Orange body, green cup for leaves, Tiffany stem vase.

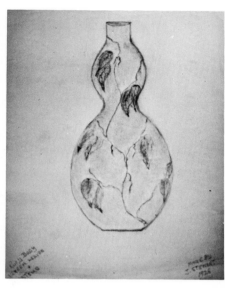

94. Made by J. Stewart 1926. Ruby body, green leaves and stems.

95. Made by J. Stewart 1926. Light ruby body, dark green cup for leaves on body and foot.

96. Made by J. A. Stewart 1926.

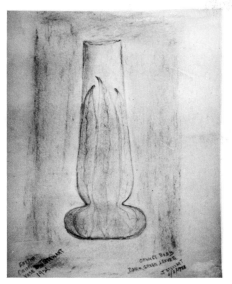

97. Egyptian Onion Vase by J. Stewart 1928. Orange body, dark green leaves, J. Stewart 1/3/1928.

98. Two J. A. Stewart sketches are superimposed here to compare with vases on display in Tiffany Furnaces before 1928.

SEVEN

DESK SETS, CANDLESTICKS, AND ACCESSORIES

Prior to 1898, most of Tiffany's metalwork was made by others from his specifications, including the stands for the vases shown in Ills. 34 and 41, all mountings for lamps and lighting fixtures, and various metal ornaments used in his interiors. Only in 1897 did he organize a foundry and metal shop as an expansion of his Corona glass furnace. The first products from this new plant appeared in New York the following year, mostly as lamps and lamp bases.

The first important exhibition of the products of the Tiffany foundry was held in London, arranged by S. Bing to promote his Salon de l'Art Nouveau in 1899, at the Grafton Galleries. Among the items shown were lamps, candelabra, inkstands, and letter and powder boxes, as well as windows, mosaics, and blown glass. The introduction to the catalogue, written by Bing, praised Tiffany and his work. This introduction was recently reprinted in full as a section in Samuel Bing's *Artistic America, Tiffany Glass and Art Nouveau,* The MIT Press, 1970. The complete list of objects exhibited is included here to indicate the

99. Tiffany metalworking shop at the Tiffany Furnaces, Corona, Long Island.

variety and types of materials being promoted by Tiffany in the last year of the nineteenth century. Although the metalwork was not illustrated in the catalogue, the descriptions of the objects are of considerable interest.

CATALOGUE OF TIFFANY'S WORKS
AT THE GRAFTON GALLERIES, LONDON, IN 1899

Favrile Blown Glass

A collection comprising both ornamental and useful objects, such as:

Vases, bowls and flower-forms, plaques, pendants for electric light, lamp- and candle-shades, wine-glasses, &c.

A variety of colours and iridescent and metallic lustres. Many forms of decoration, produced by the combination of different glasses in blowing the piece—such as the peacock feather, flower or leaf-like, wave-line and others.

Windows in Favrile Glass

1. Fish.
2. Peonies.
3. Italian Garden, from a cartoon by Louis C. Tiffany.
4. Upper section of No. 10.
5. Sheet of Favrile Glass with quartz-pebbles.
6. "Music," from a cartoon by Frank Brangwyn.
6a. The Fire-Worshippers, from a cartoon by F. S. Church.
7. Ornamental panel.
8. Fish.
9. Baptism of Christ, from a cartoon by Frank Brangwyn.
10. Window in memory of Edward T. Steel, former superintendent of schools, Philadelphia, Pennsylvania, from a cartoon by Frederic Wilson.
    Subject: Astronomy, Agriculture, Joinery, Sewing, Recreation, Architecture, Painting, Music, Chemistry, Cooking, Study, Forging.
11. In the style of a Chartres Window of the Twelfth Century.
12. Egg-plant.
13. Head of Joseph of Arimathea, from "The Entombment"—a window of Louis C. Tiffany exhibited at the World's Fair in Chicago, now in the Cathedral of St. John the Divine, New York City.

Mosaics in Favrile Glass

1. Last Supper: Altar-piece for a memorial chapel in the United States, from a cartoon by Frederic Wilson.
2. A North American Indian, part of a frieze in the Marquette Office Building, Chicago, Illinois.
3. Mantel-piece.
4. Mirror-frame.
5. Part of the frieze of the Delivery Room in the Public Library—Chicago, Illinois.

A number of samples of mosaic.

Cartoons and Sketches

1. Windows and mosaic, in the Church of St. Michael and All Angels, New York City. The five central panels are windows and those at either end are in mosaic.
2. The Fathers of the Church. A mosaic panel exhibited with the Tiffany Chapel at the World's Fair, Chicago, Illinois.

And a collection of sketches for windows, decorations, mosaic, &c.

LAMPS AND METAL WORK

1. Portable electric reading lamp in green glass and green bronze.
2. Portable electric reading lamp in repoussé metal with Favrile glass shade.
3. Portable electric reading lamp in metal inlay.
4. Portable electric reading lamp in metal inlay.
5. Portable electric reading lamp in gilt metal and natural Nautilus shell.
6. Portable electric reading lamp in green metal and leaded glass, Nautilus shell.
7. Portable oil lamp in green bronze and glass with leaded shade, dragon-fly design.
8. Portable oil lamp in silver plate and glass with crab feet.
9. Portable oil lamp in green metal and glass.
10. Portable oil lamp in silver plate and glass.
11. Portable oil lamp in metal with glass blown inside.
12. Portable oil lamp in perforated metal with glass blown inside.
13. Portable oil lamp in metal and Favrile glass.
14. Double student lamp in metal inlay with Favrile glass shade.
15. Electric standard lamp (4 lights) in metal with Favrile glass globes.
16. Small electric writing lamp in silver plate with Favrile glass shade.
17. Electric hanging lantern in perforated metal with glass blown inside.
18. Electric hanging lantern in perforated metal and glass.
19. Electric hanging lantern in metal and glass.
20. Electric hanging lantern in perforated metal with glass blown inside.
21. Large picture light in leaded glass.

22. Small picture light in leaded glass.
23. Small picture light in leaded glass.
24. Electrolier (five lights) in metal with glass blown inside.
25. Electric hanging lamp for library table in metal and leaded glass.
26. Electric hanging lamp for library table in leaded glass.
27. Electric hanging lamp for library table in leaded glass.
28. Candelabra (four lights) in metal with glass blown inside.
29. Candelabra (two lights) in metal with glass blown inside.
30. Candelabra (one light) in metal with glass blown inside.
31. Inkstand in metal with glass blown inside.
32. Inkstand in metal, wild carrot flower design.
33. Inkstand in metal, dahlia design.
34. Inkstand in metal with crab design.
35. Paper-weight in metal with crab design.
36. Letter-box in perforated metal and glass.
37. Plaque in metal inlay.
38. Plaque in metal inlay.
39. Powder-box in metal inlay.
40. Powder-box in metal inlay.
41. Powder-box in metal inlay.
42. Screen in leaded glass for spirit lamp.

* * *

Most of Tiffany's metalware was made of bronze for casting or copper for sheets or spun shapes. All items were carefully handworked by either chasing or etching and then plated or patina finished. Many items could be obtained in silver, gold, brown, or green finishes. Here is the formula for Tiffany green as supplied to me by Irving H. Levine:

Tiffany Green Patina

copper sulfate	—8 oz.
ammonium chloride	—4 oz.
sodium chloride	—4 oz.
zinc chloride	—1 oz.
acetic acid	—2 oz.
water	—1 gal.

"Use only on copper or copper-plated bronze. The addition of 1 oz. of glycerine will prevent the green from drying too fast and produce a more even color. The articles are immersed in this solution and, if the color is not uniform, the immersions are repeated as often as desired, allowing the work to dry thoroughly between immersions."

The first of the bronzes were numbered individually and stamped with the trademark of the Tiffany Glass and Decorating Company. By 1900 the numbers were already running into the tens of thousands, and an additional mark reading "Tiffany Studios, New York" was added. In 1902, the T G and D Co. mark was dropped and the numbering system was changed from individual to model numbers. The Tiffany Studios price list of October 1, 1906, reprinted in the Appendix, serves as a form of registry, since it lists the items in numerical sequence. Ills. 104 and 105 show the two systems, before and after 1902.

At first the new system was simple to follow. Lamp bases began with the number 101; hanging shades began with the number 600; fancy goods including desk sets began at 800, and candlesticks began at 1200. This price list is a fine source to check for any item that has a number corresponding to the printed description, but it is not infallible. Quite a few numbers were skipped, perhaps by accident but more likely because there were already many discontinued models. Later some of these numbers were reused for a very different kind of object.

One example of this practice is No. 1146. It was first assigned to a very large and important electric lamp, one with a large floral mosaic base and a cobweb shade, similar to oil lamp No. 146. In this case it must be assumed that somebody at Tiffany's added the extra digit to distinguish the electric lamp from the oil lamp, but later the same No. 1146 was used for an item in the "Abalone" desk set. Other examples of the duplicate use of numbers are also found when discontinued desk items were later replaced by small bronze animal weights using Nos. 889, 890, 931, 932, and 933.

To complicate the problem of the numbers still further, many collections contain some very good examples of Tiffany's metalwork stamped "Tiffany Studios" but with no number at all, and there are even some, obviously Tiffany, that have no name. If the photographs and information published here cannot help, then the problem will have to be left to an expert.

The price list of 1906 also shows that Tiffany Studios then had in stock four different desk set patterns: "Etched Metal and Glass," "Byzantine," "Zodiac," and "Bookmark." As the "Byzantine" was discontinued soon thereafter, it is the rarest of all the desk sets. The other three sets were still in stock in 1920, and a comparison of prices

100. Seventeen different inkstands photographed at Tiffany Studios in 1902. *Courtesy of Mary Tuck.*

shows they had increased by about 50 percent. For example, the "Zodiac" paper rack (No. 1009) was $12 in 1906 and $20 in 1920. Meanwhile, of course, the value of the dollar had also changed. The value of this item has not yet increased excessively over its 1920 price. In January 1971 seven items of a "Zodiac" desk set—a letter rack, inkstand, two blotter ends, calendar, letter holder, and pen tray—sold at auction in New York as a lot for $380.

A photograph (see Ill. 100) made at Tiffany Studios in 1902 shows seventeen various inkstands (their numbers correspond to the numbers in the 1906 price list). These items with their inlaid glass, mosaics, and "blown glass inside" are single items for both use and decorative effect. Ill. 102 is a powder box with a peacock feather design and inlaid mother-of-pearl. Ill. 103 shows the effect of the "blown glass inside" method, and although it has only the old number, it corresponds to No. 849 in the system of 1902. Ill. 106 shows the use of iridescent mosaic in a pen tray of swirl design, No. 1001. The paperweight in Ill. 107, which is not signed or numbered, is of metal and glass with a wave design, No. 933. The designer of these items, as well as of

101. Three-scarab inkstand No. 857, marked both TG & D Co and Tiffany Studios and numbered 21568, therefore dates between 1900 and 1902. Author's Collection.

102. Powder box, peacock feather design, is signed Tiffany Studios but has no number.

103. Inkstand, blown glass in metal, No. 849 in the price list of 1906, dates between 1900 and 1902. It is signed as shown in Ill. 104.

candlesticks and lamp bases, directly under Louis C. Tiffany, was Alvin J. Tuck. He had been hired in 1898 as designer and supervisor of the metal shop, and he remained in that capacity until 1911. Helping him with sheet metalwork and metal spinning was Thomas Conlan, employed in 1906 and remaining as master spinner until 1928.

Tiffany Studios produced and sold matched desk sets in more than fifteen patterns in all during the first two decades of the twentieth century. Every item of each set was priced and sold individually, and so there was never really a basic set although there was a minimum to what could be considered a set. The least number of pieces deemed a set was nine: blotter ends, inkstand, pen tray, paper rack, paper knife, rocker blotter, memo pad holder, stamp or utility box, and calendar. The patterns were "Pine-needle," "Grape-vine," "Zodiac," "Byzantine," "Bookmark," "Ninth Century," "Venetian," "Abalone," "American Indian," "Chinese," "Adam," "Graduate," "Royal Copper," "Louis XVI," and "Nautical." Another, only very recently identified as "Modeled Design," appears in Ill. 116. There may be still more patterns that have yet to come to our attention.

104. Signature on base of inkstand shown in Ill. 103.

105. Tiffany signature on metalware made between 1902 and 1918.

107. Paperweight, metal and glass with wave design, not signed.

106. Pen tray with mosaic and swirl design, signed Tiffany Studios.

All metalwork at Tiffany's was supposed to be signed and numbered before being finished, and there was better control over the bronzes than there was over the glass. Nevertheless, some items did get by without being signed or numbered. But there were also imitations made in the 1920s. One of the imitators, supposedly employing workmen from Tiffany's, was Riviere Studios, which produced desk sets in the "Etched Metal and Glass," "Bookmark," and "American Indian" patterns, often with no signature. These, like most other imitations, are inferior in quality.

109. Inkstand No. 847, "Etched Metal and Glass," pine-needle design, gold plated over amber opalescent glass.

ETCHED METAL AND GLASS DESK SET

THE individual beauty of this set consists in a metal overlay representing pine boughs or grape vines combined with Favrile Glass. These sets are finished in Green or Gold plated over glass of Amber and opalescent tones.

List No.	Description	Price	List No.	Description	Price
800	Utility Box	$11.00	971	Paper Clip	$ 8.00
801	Stamp Box	11.00	981	Pen Brush	8.00
844	Inkstand, large square	20.00	995	Rocker Blotter	15.00
845	Inkstand, small square	15.00	997	Blotter Corners	18.00
846	Inkstand, small round	18.00	998	Blotter Ends, 12"x19" Pad	15.00
847	Inkstand, large round	30.00	999	Blotter Ends, 19"x24" Pad	20.00
872	Letter Scales	14.00	1004	Pen Tray	10.00
903	Reading Glass	12.00	1007	Paper Rack, large	35.00
930	Paper Weight Calendar		1008	Paper Rack, small	25.00
	(Perpetual)	12.00	1010	Pen Holder	4.00
939	Calendar, large (Perpetual)	18.00	1013	Thermometer	15.00
940	Calendar, med. (Perpetual)	15.00	1019	Letter Rack	18.00
941	Calendar, small (Perpetual)	12.00	1022	Memoranda Pad, plain or	
961	Bill File	8.00		dated	16.00
968	Paper Knife, etched metal	3.00	1024	Book Ends	20.00
969	Paper Knife, etched metal		445	Lamp, $35.00. Gold	44.00
	and glass	8.00		10-inch Favrile Glass Shade	14.00

108. "Etched Metal and Glass" desk set from the Tiffany Studios' list of 1920.

ZODIAC DESK SET

FINISHED in Green Brown or Gold and ornamented with a primitive design rudely modelled, these pieces are very dignified and simple in character. The Zodiac Signs are carved in low relief on the Medallions formed by the interlacing band ornament.

List No.	Description	Price	List No.	Description	Price
802	Stamp Box	$10.00	1000	Pen Tray	$ 7.00
810	Utility Box	12.00	1009	Paper Rack, small	20.00
842	Inkstand, small	18.00	1014	Thermometer	15.00
874	Scales	14.00	1030	Paper Rack, large	35.00
928	Reading Glass 4" lens	12.00	1041	Match Stand	14.00
929	Paper Weight Calendar		1072	Inkstand, large	30.00
	(Perpetual)	9.00	1073	Inkstand for Double Desk	50.00
934	Paper Weight	5.00	1080	Paper Clip	7.00
942	Cabinet Photograph Frame	18.00	1085	Pen Brush	15.00
943	Calendar (Perpetual)	18.00	1089	Letter Rack	16.00
962	Bill File	8.00	1090	Memoranda Pad, plain or	
976	Ash Tray	6.00		dated	15.00
988	Blotter Ends, 19"x24" Pad	20.00	1091	Book Ends	18.00
990	Rocker Blotter	12.00	1093	Daily Memoranda Calendar	18.00
994	Blotter Ends, 12"x19" Pad	17.00	1095	Paper Knife	6.00
996	Blotter Corners	15.00	537	Lamp, $30.00. Gold	38.00
1010	Penholder	4.00	1587	Shade	30.00

111. "Zodiac" desk set, Tiffany Studios, price list 1920.

110. Utility box No. 800, "Etched Metal and Glass," with grapevine design; green patina over green marble opalescent glass.

112. "Zodiac" inkstand, No. 1072.

113. "Zodiac" utility box, No. 810.

115. "Bookmark" card case, No. 882, listed for $18 on the price list of 1906 but not included on the list of 1920.

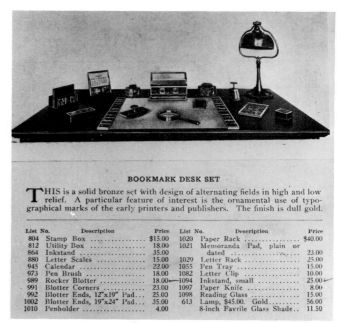

BOOKMARK DESK SET

THIS is a solid bronze set with design of alternating fields in high and low relief. A particular feature of interest is the ornamental use of typographical marks of the early printers and publishers. The finish is dull gold.

List No.	Description	Price	List No.	Description	Price
804	Stamp Box	$15.00	1020	Paper Rack	$40.00
812	Utility Box	18.00	1021	Memoranda Pad, plain or	
864	Inkstand	35.00		dated	23.00
880	Letter Scales	15.00	1029	Letter Rack	25.00
945	Calendar	22.00	1055	Pen Tray	15.00
973	Pen Brush	18.00	1082	Letter Clip	10.00
989	Rocker Blotter	18.00	1094	Inkstand, small	25.00
991	Blotter Corners	23.00	1097	Paper Knife	8.00
992	Blotter Ends, 12"x19" Pad	25.00	1098	Reading Glass	15.00
1002	Blotter Ends, 19"x24" Pad	35.00	613	Lamp, $45.00. Gold	56.00
1010	Penholder	4.00		8-inch Favrile Glass Shade	11.50

114. "Bookmark" desk set, price list of 1920.

116. Inkstand signed Tiffany Studios 1112, "Modeled Design" not included in either the list of 1906 or that of 1920. Other items of this set in the Author's Collection are blotter ends/No. 1110, paper rack No. 1116, pen tray, No. 1113, rocker blotter No. 1115, and letter clip No. 1119. There were seventeen items in this pattern, numbered from 1110 to 1126.

ABALONE DESK SET

THIS is a bronze set of beautiful workmanship, highly finished in soft gold with incised lines of tonal color following the conventionalized pattern of the design. This ornament surrounds discs of the natural Abalone shell embedded in the metal.

List No.	Description	Price	List No.	Description	Price
1151	Paper Rack	$35.00	1166	Calendar (Perpetual)	$20.00
1152	Blotter Ends, 19"x24" Pad	30.00	1167	Thermometer	18.00
1153	Blotter Ends, 12"x19" Pad	23.00	1169	Memoranda Pad, plain or	
1154	Blotter Corner	25.00		dated	22.00
1156	Letter Rack	25.00	1170	Letter Scales	18.00
1157	Inkstand	25.00	1171	Photograph Frame	25.00
1158	Stamp Box	16.00	1173	Book Ends	28.00
1159	Pen Tray	14.00	1176	Utility Box	17.00
1160	Pen Brush	16.00	1178	Reading Glass	12.00
1163	Paper Knife	8.00	1179	Photograph Frame (Cabinet)	25.00
1164	Rocker Blotter	15.00	1010	Pen Holder	4.00
1165	Letter Clip	8.00	604	Lamp—gold only	75.00
			1928	Shade	70.00

117. "Abalone" desk set, list of 1920. The abstract design is based on grapes and grapevines, with inlaid abalone shell disks serving as grapes.

AMERICAN INDIAN DESK SET

I N this set is embodied the Art of the American Indian The motifs chosen
are the Seasons, symbolized by the Serpent, the Frog, the Bird and the Rain
and Storm. The connected circles represent the Flight of Time. The set is of
Bronze, finished in Green, Brown or Gold.

List No.	Description	Price	List No.	Description	Price
1180	Blotter Ends, 12"x19" Pad...	$18.00	1189	Paper Knife	$ 6.00
1181	Blotter Ends, 19"x24" Pad...	25.00	1190	Letter Clip	9.00
1183	Inkstand	25.00	1191	Rocker Blotter	12.00
1184	Stamp Box	15.00	1192	Utility Box	15.00
1185	Pen Tray	10.00	1193	Letter Rack	16.00
1186	Paper Rack	25.00	1194	Match Stand	14.00
1187	Calendar (Perpetual)	15.00	1195	Reading Glass	12.00
1188	Memoranda Pad, plain or dated	17.00	1010	Penholder	4.00

119. "American Indian" desk set, first introduced by Tiffany Studios in 1909. This is in the list of 1920.

118. "Abalone" perpetual calendar No. 1166.

120. "American Indian" inkstand No. 1183.

NINTH CENTURY DESK SET

WITH its bands of carved ornament and fields of deeply cut strap work, this set is one of the most elaborate. Small animals are introduced in the design as substitutes for the Ninth Century grotesque forms which are usually puzzling and unattractive. The set is finished in gold, mounted with jewels.

List No.	Description	Price	List No.	Description	Price
515	Lamp and Shade, Gold only	$300.00	1628	Rocker Blotter	$20.00
1618	Calendar, small	20.00	1629	Pen Brush	20.00
1619	Reading Glass	12.00	1630	Ash Tray	12.00
1620	Letter Rack	20.00	1631	Paper Weight	9.00
1621	Inkstand	35.00	1632	Calendar, large	28.00
1622	Blotter Ends, 19"x24" Pad	35.00	1633	Paper Knife	8.00
1623	Blotter Ends, 12"x19" Pad	30.00	1634	Blotter Corners	30.00
1624	Stamp Box	25.00	1637	Letter Clip	12.00
1625	Paper Rack	40.00	1639	Memoranda Pad, plain or	
1626	Pen Tray	18.00		dated	25.00
1627	Letter Scales	20.00	1697	Cabinet Photograph Frame	28.00
1010	Penholder	4.00	1699	Inkstand, small	25.00

121. "Ninth Century" desk set, list of 1920.

122. Inkstand No. 1621 with green glass jewels. The "Ninth Century" set could be purchased with pink, green, or blue jewels. These are often broken or missing today.

VENETIAN DESK SET

THIS set is decorated with fields of richly chased ornament relieved by a deeply carved band of ermines at the base of each piece. The style of decoration was used extensively in the Sixteenth Century by Venetian craftsmen in making tooled leather objects. Reproduced in metal this ornament gives the rich effect found in East Indian metal work. The finish is dull gold.

List No.	Description	Price	List No.	Description	Price
515	Lamp and Shade, Gold only	$300.00	1685	Paper Knife	$10.00
1640	Blotter Ends, 12"x19" Pad..	30.00	1686	Pen Brush	20.00
1641	Inkstand	40.00	1688	Thermometer	20.00
1642	Pen Tray	20.00	1689	Ash Tray	12.00
1643	Letter Rack	25.00	1690	Letter Scales	25.00
1644	Paper Rack	40.00	1691	Memoranda Pad, plain or	
1645	Stamp Box	25.00		dated	30.00
1646	Rocker Blotter	20.00	1693	Letter Clip	12.00
1647	Paper Weight	12.00	1694	Blotter Corners	40.00
1648	Calendar	25.00	1696	Blotter Ends, 19"x24" Pad..	40.00
1010	Penholder	4.00	1698	Reading Glass	15.00
1684	Match Stand	22.00	1700	Inkstand, small	25.00

23 1683 Book Ends   25.00

123. "Venetian" desk set, list of 1920.

124. "Venetian" blotter ends No. 1640 showing the band of ermines.

CHINESE DESK SET

THE Ancient Symbolism of China is quaintly expressed in this unique set. The Modern Art has adapted the motifs found in the bronzes of the Chou dynasty, incorporating many of the Antique forms and symbols. The set is executed in Bronze, finished in Green, Brown or Gold.

List No.	Description	Price	List No.	Description	Price
1751	Blotter Ends, 19"x24" Pad...	$25.00	1759	Paper Knife	$ 6.00
1753	Inkstand	32.00	1760	Rocker Blotter	12.00
1754	Stamp Box	18.00	1761	Cabinet Photograph Frame	40.00
1755	Pen Tray	12.00	1762	Letter Clip	9.00
1756	Paper Rack	35.00	535	Lamp, $45.00. Gold	56.00
1757	Calendar (Perpetual)	20.00	1588	Lamp Shade	
1758	Memoranda Pad, plain or dated	18.00	1763	Inkstand, double	20.00
1010	Penholder	4.00	1764	Match stand	18.00

125. "Chinese" desk set, list of 1920.

126. "Chinese" paper rack No. 1756.

ADAM DESK SET

THIS set is finished in dull rich gold. The exquisite workmanship and delicacy of detail are in harmony with the best efforts of the Adam period.

List No.	Description	Price	List No.	Description	Price
1775	Blotter Ends, 19"x24" Pad...	$28.00	1782	Calendar (Perpetual)	$20.00
1776	Blotter Ends, 12"x19" Pad...	23.00	1783	Paper Clip	10.00
1777	Inkstand	30.00	1784	Rocker Blotter	16.00
1778	Pen Tray	17.00	1785	Memoranda Pad, plain or dated	22.00
1779	Paper Rack	30.00	1786	Photograph Frame	25.00
1780	Paper Knife	7.00	539	Lamp—Gold only	50.00
1781	Utility Box	23.00	1412	Shade—Metal and Glass	45.00

127. "Adam" desk set, list of 1920.

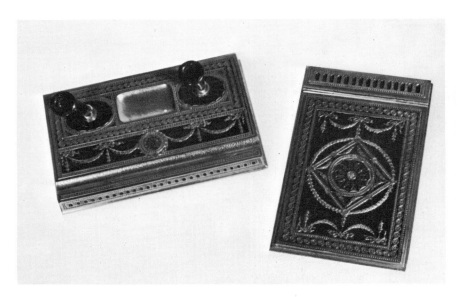

128. "Adam" memoranda pad, No. 1785, and double pen holder, No. 2108, both decorated with green enamel on gold-plated finish.

GRADUATE DESK SET

THE distinguishing feature of this set consists in its simplicity of line and decoration. The pieces are finished in gold, brown or green with inlay of soft color tones.

List No.	Description	Price	List No.	Description	Price
1791	Photograph Frame ... *12.*	$18.00	1803	Paper Rack	30.00
1792	Paper Weight Calendar		1804	Calendar (Perpetual)	12.00
	(Perpetual)	10.00	1805	Paper Clip	8.00
1793	Reading Glass	10.00	1806	Scales	15.00
1794	Pen Brush	12.00	1807	Book Ends	16.00
1795	Blotter Ends, 12″x19″ Pad...	15.00	1808	Pad Holder—plain or dated..	15.00
1796	Blotter Ends, 19″x24″ Pad. *20.* *22.00*		1809	Bill File	*8.00*
1797	Stamp Box	12.00	1810	Daily Memoranda Pad.......	22.00
1798	Pen Tray	10.00	1811	Paper Rack, large	35.00
1799	Utility Box	15.00	1812	Letter Rack	15.00
1800	Paper Knife	6.00	1813	Inkstand, small	*18.00* *15*
1801	Inkstand, large	18.00	1814	Match Stand	15.00
1802	Rocker Blotter ... *10.* ...	*12.00*	558	Lamp, $45. Gold..........	56.00
1010	Pen Holder	4.00		12-inch Favrile Glass Shade.	19.00

129. "Graduate" desk set, list of 1920.

LOUIS XVI DESK SET

LOVERS of French Art will find in this set an expression of the exquisite delicacy of this Period.

List No.	Description	Price
1820	Blotter ends; 12″x19″ Pad	$25.00
1822	Pen Tray	15.00
1823	Utility Box	25.00
1824	Paper Knife	8.00
1826	Paper Rack	40.00
1827	Ink Stand	30.00
1828	Pad Holder, plain or engagement	25.00
1829	Rocker Blotter	18.00
1830	Calendar	20.00
538	Lamp	50.00
1413	14-in. Silk Shade	45.00

130. "Louis XVI" desk set, list of 1920.

NAUTICUAL DESK SET

THIS set as its name implies embodies in its design varied motifs of the Sea. Executed in soft green tones, it is of unusual interest.

List No.	Description	Price
1840	Blotter Ends, 19"x24" Pad	$28.00
1842	Ink Stand	28.00
1843	Pen Tray	12.00
1844	Paper Knife	7.00
1845	Utility Box	27.00
1846	Rocker Blotter	15.00
1847	Pad Holder	22.00
1848	Calendar	20.00
1849	Paper Rack	35.00
612	Lamp	38.00
	Favrile Glass Shade 12 in. diam.	19.00
1841. Blotter Ends 12x19 Pad		22.00

131. "Nautical" desk set, list of 1920.

132. Utility box, No. 1845.

133. Ladies' inkstand, No. 1601, pink enamel on gold-plated bronze, not included on list of either 1906 or 1920.

134. Tiffany Studios photograph of five inkstands, as shown in the original photo catalogue. They were priced as follows:

1039—$20.00	1073—$50.00
1036— 20.00	1038— 85.00
1037— 30.00	

Candelabra and candlesticks were featured by Tiffany Studios in its metal showrooms at all times, and they are as distinctive and characteristic of the Art Nouveau style as any other items of glass, metal, or pottery. Even before he could produce them in quantity, Tiffany designed some very elegant candlesticks for the chapel he displayed in Chicago in 1893. Originally there were six on the altar and two alongside the lectern. Details of the bases of two of the candlesticks on the altar can be seen in Ills. 135 and 136, which show the intricacy of the workmanship—the fine detailing of the metalcraft and the setting of the stones (in this case, quartz pebbles). This high quality of craftsmanship was a model to those who followed. Here, in the design of these candlesticks by Tiffany, is certainly the source for the "Ninth Century" and "Venetian" desk sets, as well as for all the Tiffany Studios candelabra.

One all-bronze candlestick in my collection (see Ill. 137) is some-

135 and **136**. Bases of two of the candlesticks designed by Louis C. Tiffany for the altar of the Tiffany Chapel in the Columbian Exposition in Chicago in 1893. *Chick Hardy photos.*

what of a mystery even to me, probably because Tiffany himself designed it and may even have helped to make it. There is no doubt about its authenticity, but its signature and numbers do not conform to any known system. The signature (Ill. 138) is Tiffany's autograph and the number is 68. The foot is a lily pad; the cup is red enamel. At the very least this was a special order.

Allowing for such exceptions, the signatures and numbers on candlesticks are similar to those of other metal products, with the sequence beginning at 1200. Ill. 139 shows an early example, before 1902, with the number 22324. It is similar to the one that was item No. 28 in the London exhibit of 1899. This particular style appears to have been discontinued before 1906.

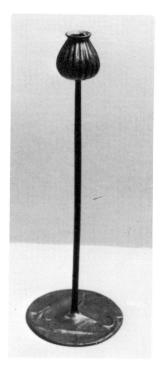

137. Candlestick with signature of Louis C. Tiffany; height 18″. Author's Collection.

Comparison of Original Prices of Tiffany Candlesticks

Number	Type	1906	1930
1200	1-light root	4.00	12.00
1201	1-light four-legged	7.00	16.00
1203	1-light leaf	6.00	14.00
1205	1-light bamboo	7.00	12.00
1213	1-light plain	4.00	12.00
1230	2-light bud	8.00	18.00
1232	2-light fleur-de-lis	12.00	22.00
1290	6-light, in a row	24.00	50.00

138. Signature on base of candlestick shown in Ill. 137.

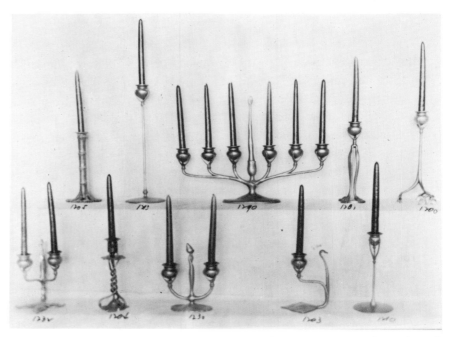

140. Photograph of ten candlesticks numbered in the 1200 series, taken from the original Tiffany Studios Photo Catalogue. The prices were set in 1920, and were later reduced for special sales in the 1930s. They ranged from $12 to $50.

139. Four-light candlestick, green glass blown into bronze, signed Tiffany Studios 22324, dates between 1900 and 1902.

In the Kovels' *Complete Antiques Price List,* Second Edition, 1970, No. 1230 is priced at $50 and No. 1232 at $80, but the prices have since increased further. A pair of bronze candlesticks marked "Tiffany Studios New York 1213" sold at auction in New York on April 23, 1971, for $150. It must also be remembered that for a twenty-year period, from 1938 to 1958, Tiffany Studios bronzes were considered to be worthless. Many were junked for scrap during World War II, and I can remember that as recently as 1956, it was possible to buy almost any of them for two dollars apiece.

Most, but not all, Tiffany Studios candlesticks were signed. Many had interchangeable caps, some of which are described at the end of the 1906 price list. The marks, always on the base, were the T G and D Co or the T S monogram (Ill. 141), or the words Tiffany Studios, New York. The twelve original Tiffany Studios photographs, Ills. 142 through 153, published here for the first time (through the courtesy of

141. Tiffany Studios monogram mark on No. 1230, two-light bud candlestick in the author's collection.

142–153. ORIGINAL PHOTOGRAPHS OF CANDLESTICKS MADE AT TIFFANY STUDIOS. *Courtesy of Mary Tuck.*

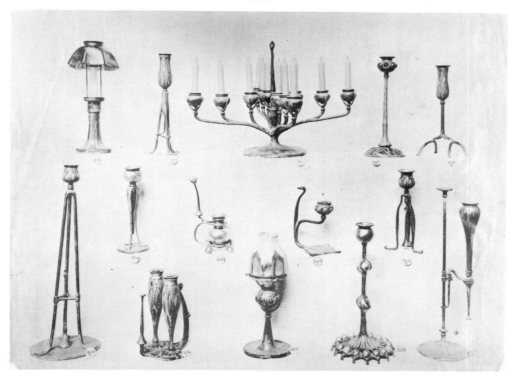

142

Alvin J. Tuck's daughter, Mary Tuck), should help to identify unmarked examples. According to Miss Tuck, most of these were designed by her father except for the "Wild Carrot" base, Ill. 147, which was designed by Louis C. Tiffany. These photographs also show the variety of effects obtained at Tiffany's by the addition of different mounting to hold shades or prisms and thus to change candlesticks into candle lamps.

Candlestick designs were among the most successful achievements of the Tiffany firm. In form, the candlesticks are often similar to the flower-form vases of blown Tiffany glass, but they clearly express the stronger nature of their metal and the difference in the forming process. Consistent with the principles of Art Nouveau, they were inspired by and evoked the growth forms found in nature. They come in gold, green, brown, or silver, and were frequently enhanced by the use of iridescent glass jewels or balls. The Tiffany photographs indicate that they were not normally sold in pairs.

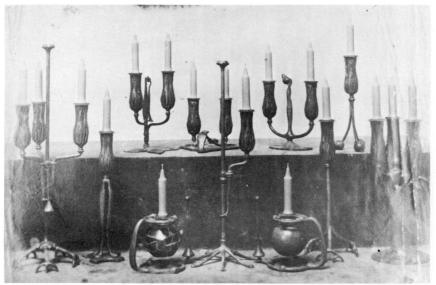

143

144

145

146

147

148

149

150

151

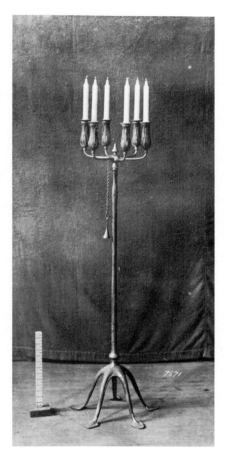

152

153

The decade from 1906 until 1916 was one of continual expansion for Tiffany Studios when they were constantly increasing the number of items to be used as gifts. There were jewel and cigar boxes, picture frames, planters, ash receivers, and spun metal compotes and dishes that could be obtained in patterns to match various desk sets or be enjoyed singly. The model numbers, including lamps and lampshades, ran to over two thousand. The Tiffany photographic catalogue and price list in the author's collection, Ills. 154 to 161, gives an idea of the variety of gift items and accessories made and sold by Tiffany Studios. The interior of the metal showroom in the Tiffany Studios building at Forty-fifth Street and Madison Avenue, New York (Ill. 162), shows how they were displayed for sale. There even the keys to the cabinets (Ill. 163) bore the T S monogram. The real splendor of these showrooms can be sensed from the character of the stairway at the main entrance, Ill. 164.

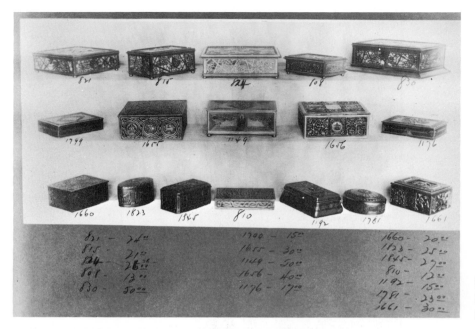

154. Assortment of boxes shown in the Tiffany Studios Photo Catalogue. The prices in 1920 ranged from $12 to $50.

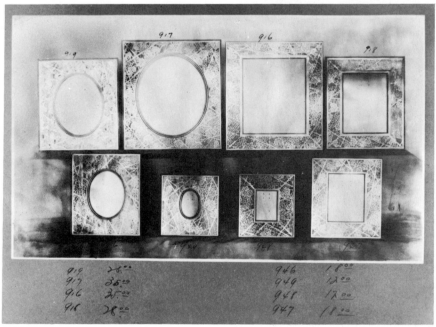

155. Assortment of picture frames, shown in the Tiffany Studios Photo Catalogue.

156. Assortment of planters, one of which, No. 835 (*lower left*), was out of stock and therefore "discontinued."

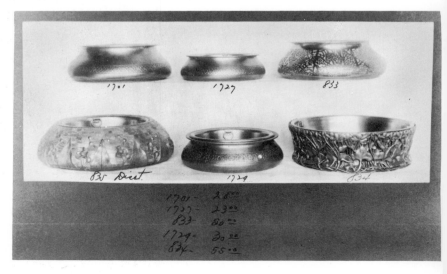

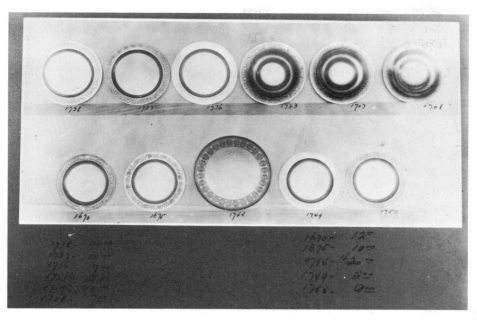

157. Spun metal dishes with etched or inlaid patterns, as shown in the same photographic catalogue.

During this period of expansion there was absolutely no decline in the quality of workmanship—no expense was spared to acquire the finest possible materials and to finish them to perfection. This policy continued as long as Louis C. Tiffany was actively guiding the various industries that he had founded. Over two hundred designers and skilled craftsmen were then employed, and the objects they turned out were sold in a carefully selected number of outlets. In New York City only Tiffany Studios and Tiffany and Company carried the line. Other retailers included Marshall Field in Chicago, Nieman Marcus in Dallas, Shreve's in San Francisco, and the Salon de l'Art Nouveau in Paris. Also, there were many private special orders, handled directly through the office of the Studios, that were made for and shipped directly to specific clients.

It is because of the special order services of Tiffany Studios that no list of Tiffany products can ever be complete and definitive. Many of the items made on special order were stamped "Tiffany Studios, New York," but did not carry a model number and were recorded only on the bill of sale. Many others were not marked or signed, and no record of these has survived. There are important bronzes, like the one in Ill. 165, that do not appear in any catalogue or price list of the times.

158. Variety of footed metal compotes similar to those in Ill. 157, from the Tiffany Studios Photo Catalogue.

159. Ash receivers, some with glass liners, some adjustable in height, as shown in the Tiffany Studios Photo Catalogue.

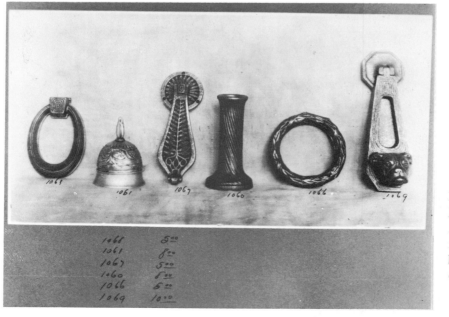

160. Small bronzes—door knockers, bell, ring, hatpin holder—ranged in price from $5 to $10 and used numbers assigned after 1906 but before 1918. *Tiffany Studios Photo Catalogue.*

161. Animal paperweights of solid bronze were priced from $4 to $15. *Tiffany Studios Photo Catalogue.*

163. Key with Tiffany Studios monogram made for the cabinets at Tiffany Studios. Author's Collection.

162. The metal showroom at Tiffany Studios, as shown in a promotion booklet in 1913.

164. Main stairway at the entrance to Tiffany Studios, from a 1913 booklet.

During the war (from 1916 to 1918), production was severely curtailed. Then followed a major reorganization, which included, in 1919, the retirement from active participation of both Louis C. Tiffany and Arthur J. Nash, although the two men retained their titles of president and vice-president, respectively. Tiffany Furnaces was incorporated separately under the direction of A. Douglas Nash, and Tiffany Studios was managed by Joseph Briggs. The sumptuous building on Madison Avenue was vacated and the showrooms moved to smaller quarters.

Tiffany Studios retained the entire stock of glass and bronzes that had been made during the peak years of production, and therefore had a tremendous inventory. For two decades they needed only to make windows, leaded glass lampshades, and mosaics to continue in operation. When they were finally liquidated in 1938, there were still several warehouses full of merchandise that was sold at auction. Some of this, including several tons of unused glass and the photographic catalogue used in part to illustrate this volume, was still in storage in 1964. No desk sets, candlesticks, cast bronzes for lamp bases, or accessories were manufactured and stamped "Tiffany Studios" after 1918.

Tiffany Furnaces, Inc., began to produce a new line with a new signature and a new numbering system in 1919, and continued in operation until 1928. The change in style from Tiffany Studios to Tiffany Furnaces was not a radical one, and many of the same craftsmen were retained. Nevertheless there was a decline in quality through the effort to cut costs.

Jimmy Stewart stayed on as gaffer in the glassblowing department; Thomas Conlam was in charge of metalwork. And in 1921 Patricia Gay was persuaded to come back to work to enhance the new metal with her enamels (Ill. 166). Patricia Gay, daughter of the painter Edward Gay, and her brother, Duncan Gay, had both begun to work for Tiffany before 1900. An ardent suffragette, Miss Gay had left Tiffany to enlist in the Women's Camouflage Corps during World War I. She accepted the offer made in a letter by Nash, and remained in charge of enameling until 1928. The metalwork produced by the Tiffany Furnaces, Inc., was much more extensively decorated with varicolored enamels than had been the case with that made for Tiffany Studios.

A comparison of the bud vases in Ills. 167 and 168 highlights the similarities and differences of work before and after 1919. In all these pieces, the blown glass is made and signed in the same way, with the initials "L. C. T." But both from the metal and the sources, we know that the five vases in Ill. 167 were from Tiffany Studios; the one in Ill. 168, signed as shown in Ill. 169, is of a later date. Though the shape and proportions are similar, they are not identical. The later one is simpler, more conventional, and actually lighter in weight, since the metal was all spun and no cast elements were used. This should not be taken to imply that no casting was done. The footed compote in Ill. 170 has cast feet, and several of the items shown in the promotion leaflets (Ills. 171–174) are listed as "heavy cast bronze," including the lamp, No. 22, and the jewel case, No. 125, in Ill. 174.

Some of the designs introduced in the twenties are simpler and more angular than those of the prior decades, yet they never went all the way into the Art Deco style except for a few lamps designed by Patricia Gay. Desk sets and accessories were produced under A. Douglas Nash in the hope of getting a wider distribution than had been achieved by Tiffany Studios. He worked through more normal channels, using wholesalers and any retailer who wished to carry the line.

165. Bronze vase with Art Nouveau relief, signed "Tiffany Studios."

167. Five different bud vases, blown glass with bronze bases, as shown in the Tiffany Studios Photo Catalogue.

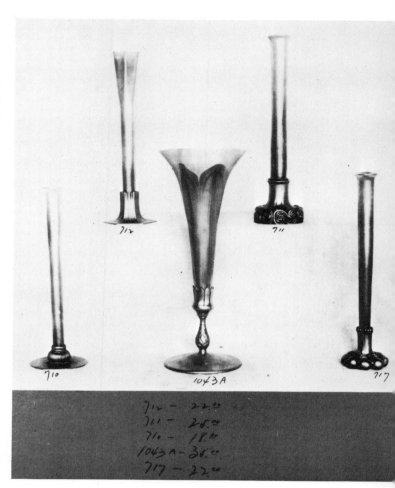

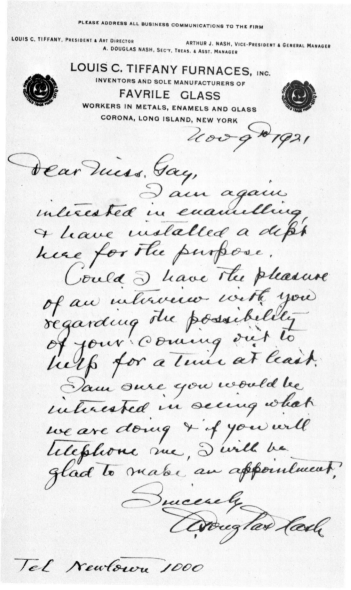

166. Letter of November 9, 1921, from A. Douglas Nash to Patricia Gay. *Courtesy of Mrs. Dorothy Gay Gordon.*

168. Bud vase, blown glass with enamel on metal base signed "Louis C. Tiffany Furnaces, Inc., Favrile."

169. Base of the vase shown in Ill. 168.

170. Bronze three-footed compote, etched gold finish, marked "Tiffany Furnaces 409." Author's Collection.

171–174. ILLUSTRATIONS FROM A SERIES OF PROMOTION LEAFLETS USED BY TIFFANY FURNACES IN THE 1920S.

A few suggestions of Desk Set articles. This set is made of heavy cast bronze with enamel inlay. The set comprises 28 individual articles. Those shown in the cut are as follows:

No. 351—Rocker Blotter
No. 352—Pen Tray
No. 353—Paper Rack
No. 355B—Blotter Ends
No. 356—Calendar
No. 357—Inkwell
No. 359—Paper Knife
No. 369—Lamp

Manufactured by
LOUIS C. TIFFANY FURNACES, Inc.
Corona, Long Island, N. Y.

171

No. 651—Clock. Heavy cast bronze with enamel inlay in various colors and finishes.

No. 38—Candlesticks. Designed to match above clock.

The small vases are unusual examples of Favrile Glass of a purely decorative character.

Manufactured by
LOUIS C. TIFFANY FURNACES, Inc.
Corona, Long Island, N. Y.

172

No. 22—Lamp. Base of heavy cast bronze with enamel inlay to harmonize with the Favrile Glass shade.

No. 159—11″ Flower Vase. See No. 158, Plate 4.

No. 129—Puff Box. Gold Favrile Glass box, with enamel cover in delicate colors.

No. 125—Jewel Case. Heavy cast bronze with Azurite enamel inlay, gold finish, supplied with two plush-covered trays.

No. 31—Hand Mirror. Favrile Glass back with carved leaf motif, mounted in metal.

No. 123—Bronze Utility Box with delicate colored enamel cover.

Manufactured by
LOUIS C. TIFFANY FURNACES, Inc.
Corona, Long Island, N. Y.

173

An intimate group of articles suitable for table decoration.

No. 158—17″ Flower Vase made in gold or blue lustres or tinted opalescent with suitably finished metal base.

No. 500—12″ Comport made in similar colors.

No. 502S—Card Tray. Favrile Glass center with carved border motif, mounted in metal with enamel inlay.

No. 309—Card Tray. Bronze with inlayed enameled jewels.

No. 372—Engagement Pad. Heavy cast bronze with enamel inlay.

Manufactured by
LOUIS C. TIFFANY FURNACES, Inc.
Corona, Long Island, N. Y.

174

Tiffany himself was not pleased, but he allowed his name to be used under this arrangement for eight years. Then, in 1928, a year before the stock market crash, Louis C. Tiffany withdrew his financial support of the Tiffany Furnaces and prohibited the use of his name. From 1928 until 1931, Nash tried to keep the glass furnaces going on his own, but he failed. The blown glass that was finished in these last few years was marked either "ADNA" for A. Douglas Nash or simply "NASH." After 1928, metal stands or other related objects of metal would not have been marked at all.

Tiffany Studios continued to operate even after the death of its founder in 1933, but it could exist only as long as Joseph Briggs survived, and that was until 1938. Many have speculated as to whether Tiffany Studios could have survived the Depression had Tiffany's will been different. As Jimmy Stewart expressed it, "He left us only his 'name.'"

EIGHT

LAMPS AND FIXTURES

Louis C. Tiffany was once reputed to have said that his lamps were a by-product of his windows. This is true only to the extent that the opalescent glass Tiffany originated for use in tiles and windows was equally, and sometimes more, effective when used with artificial illlumination. From his earliest experiments in interior decoration Tiffany showed an interest in the control of light, both natural and artificial, and the use of glass for diffusion of light. Many of the interiors shown in *Rebel in Glass,* from the Seventh Regiment Armory of 1880 to the Havemeyer House in 1890, make this quite clear. In 1885 Tiffany had worked side by side with Thomas A. Edison in the Lyceum Theatre in New York, the first theater ever to have electric footlights. This theater also had Tiffany electric sconces that were described as "like fire in monster emeralds," a description that also fits some of his later lamps, especially those using green turtleback tiles.

In 1893 Tiffany sent two great hanging fixtures to the Chicago Fair for exhibition. These were the ancestors of Tiffany lamps. One was

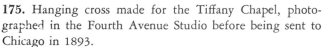

175. Hanging cross made for the Tiffany Chapel, photographed in the Fourth Avenue Studio before being sent to Chicago in 1893.

176. Electrolier illustrated in Tiffany Studios booklet of 1901.

the hanging cross for the Tiffany Chapel (Ill. 175); the other was the sanctuary lantern for the Church of the Covenant in Boston (Ill. 177). Both have lights concealed behind glass jewels. The evolution of the Tiffany lamp took place in the years immediately following. By 1898 the hanging fixture had been combined with the use of blown and leaded glass globes (Ill. 176), and Tiffany Studios was selling refinished student lamps (Ill. 179) and blown glass oil lamps (Ills. 180–185).

In 1898 when Cecilia Waern visited the Tiffany plant, she wrote, in an article for *The Studio,* of her reaction to the blown glass globes made for hanging fixtures. "For electric lights the large simple drops and eggs seem to me to be unsurpassed in beauty and fitness. It is delightful to prowl round in the lamp-room and watch the shifting effects brought out by moving the electric lights from one globe to another. These effects may be delicate—a silvery globe with a slight pattern of trailing reddish threads, and the faintest gleam of green playing round the pearly film that clouds some parts of the globe. Or they may be strong, blood-red marbles, veined with gold. They have always, somehow, the reserve and chastity of a priceless material."

The Tiffany lamp as it is known today, with its heavy bronze base and intricately worked glass shade, did not exist before 1899. In that year at least three of the still-popular Tiffany lamp types were introduced. They were the nautilus (Ills. 186 and 187), the dragonfly, and the Tyler scroll (Ill. 195). The nautilus and the dragonfly lamps were included in the exhibition of Art Nouveau in London in 1899; the noted sculptor, Louis A. Gudebrod (1872–1961) of Meriden, Connecticut, was commissioned by Tiffany to design the "mermaid" base for the nautilus lamp (Ill. 188).

Tiffany lamps could be found in two areas of the Paris Exposition of 1900: in the United States Pavilion (Ill. 50) and in Bing's Art Nouveau (Ills. 189 and 190). In 1902 in Turin, Italy, Tiffany won more prizes for his lamps, particularly the 18-light pond lily design (model 383).

The booklet "Bronze Lamps" of 1904 (Ills. 191 to 194) and the "Price List" of October 1, 1906 (Appendix 1), provide the key to the numbering system of Tiffany lamps. For the bronze bases made in Tiffany Furnaces, the numbers follow the same system as Tiffany bronzes. In some cases the model number includes the shade or shades; in other cases it does not. The scarab lamp (Ill. 14) and the nautilus lamp (Ill. 187) have the T G and D Co monogram and pre-1902 system of numbers. After 1902, the model number was stamped on the base or base plate of the lamp. If the shade had a separate or different number, it usually was stamped into the metal inside the bottom rim of the shade. The name and number also might be applied by the addition of a metal plate inside the shade. Only the metal, never the glass, is marked in leaded shades. Only blown glass shades were marked and numbered on the glass.

There were over five hundred different designs for lamp bases and over five hundred different designs for lampshades produced by Tiffany Studios. It is not likely that any one collection will include all these, or even that any one book can publish a complete list. The great variety of sizes, shapes, and kinds of lamps sold by Tiffany during the first decade of the twentieth century can best be seen in a collection of original photos assembled by Alvin J. Tuck between 1898 and 1911, which are published here (Ills. 195 through 236) for the first time.

177. Sanctuary lamp designed by J. A. Holzer, made by Tiffany. It was exhibited in Chicago in 1893, and now is in the Church of the Covenant in Boston, Massachusetts.

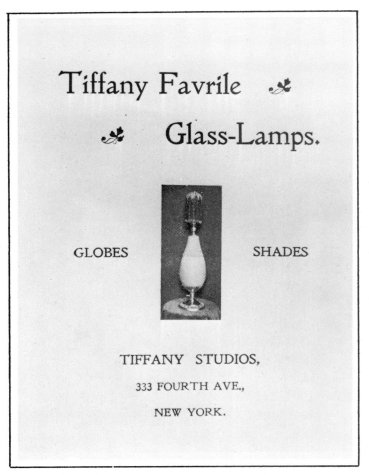

178. Title page of Tiffany Favrile lamps booklet of 1898.

179. Student lamp in the booklet of 1898.

180–185. SIX OIL, OR KEROSENE, LAMPS BY TIFFANY, AS ILLUSTRATED IN AN 1898 BOOKLET.

180

181

182

183

184

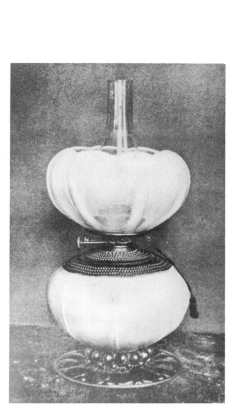

185

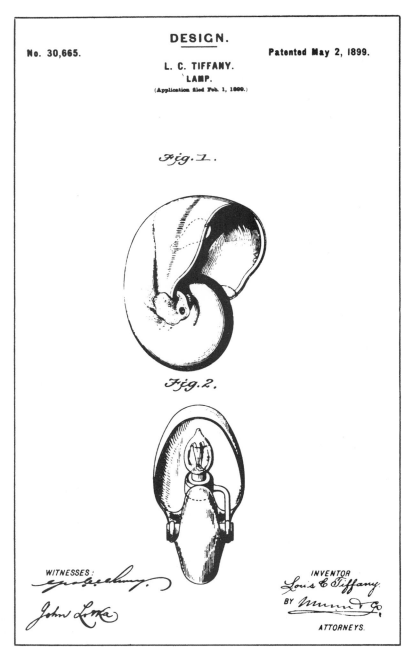

187. Nautilus lamp with leaded glass shade as exhibited in London in 1899.

186. Patent of May 2, 1899, for the nautilus lamp designed by Louis C. Tiffany.

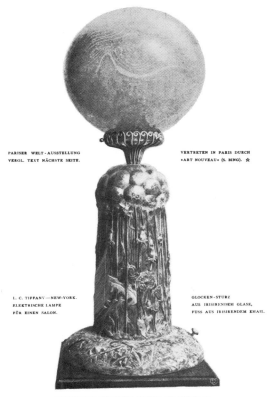

189. Tiffany electric lamp exhibited in Paris in 1900 as part of S. Bing's "Art Nouveau Bing." The base is bronze and enamel, "Dandelion" pattern; the globe is blown iridescent glass.

188. Nautilus lamp with "mermaid" base designed by Louis A. Gudebrod, illustrated in Tiffany Studios booklet of 1901.

190. Tiffany oil lamp also exhibited in Paris in 1900.

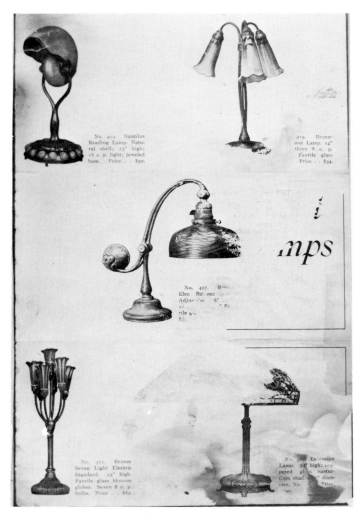

191. Page from the booklet "Bronze Lamps," Tiffany Studios 1904, showing Nos. 402, 319, 417, 311, and 367.

192. Page from "Bronze Lamps," showing No. 382, shade No. 1454, No. 373 (with shade 1524), No. 187, and No. 419.

It is virtually impossible to determine how many of each model were made. Some are fairly common, but others were unique. Where numbers are indicated on the Tuck photos, it is interesting to check the descriptions on the price list of 1906. Ills. 205 and 212, for example, represent a type of Tiffany panel lampshade that is almost unknown and, without a signature, would be suspected as the work of other than the Tiffany firm. These photos now can dispel any doubts. They also show what kinds and sizes of shades may be used on various bases.

193. Page from "Bronze Lamps" showing Nos. 328, 300, 225 (with shade 1496), 129 and 179 (with shade 1473).

194. Page from "Bronze Lamps" showing Nos. 342, 441, 119, 215, and 305.

Tiffany lamps have many features that make them extremely desirable. They are useful as lamps with bulbs of varying intensity, as the opalescent glass, whether blown or leaded, diffuses light evenly and pleasantly. They are well engineered and sturdily constructed. The cast bronze bases have sufficient weight to hold the lamps steadily, the fittings are all tight, the finest wiring was used, and the leaded glass shades were fitted and constructed so that they rarely broke unless carelessly handled or dropped. Above all else, the aesthetic qualities distinguish lamps by Tiffany from those of his competitors. Each one is a complete work of art coordinated in proportion of base and shades. Although, in some, bases and shades are interchangeable, any such transfers must be made carefully—with an eye for shape, size, and proportion.

Among the several types of Tiffany lamps, a preference for one type over another is often a purely personal matter. In the most general way, these lamps can be classified as follows:

1. Student lamps with blown glass shades
2. Lamps with blown glass base and shade
3. Bronze lamp bases with blown glass shades
4. Bronze lamp bases with bronze shades
5. Bronze bases with leaded glass shades, either geometric or naturalistic designs

Add to these categories the variations resulting from the use of mosaics, turtleback tiles, prisms, different finishes, seashells, and linenfold or fabric glass, and there is a lot to choose from in Tiffany lamps.

By far the most popular of all Tiffany lamps are those frequently called "lily," even though this name is properly applied only to those with pond-lily bases, list Nos. 381, 382, 383, and 385. Since these have "drop clusters of blossom shades," all Tiffany lamps with blossom shades are now popularly known as "lilies" and the shades are called "lily shades." These shades, originally produced in great quantities in many colors and sold at $2.50 each, are now not to be found anywhere for any amount of money. Many collectors have lamps with one or more of the shades cracked, mended, or missing and cannot replace them.

The first electric Tiffany lamp with a drop cluster of blossom shades, exhibited in Paris in 1900, created a sensation. It was noted that this was the first use of electric light to point down in a way that was not possible with an exposed flame. Two years later, in Turin, Italy, Tiffany took top honors for his eighteen-light pond-lily lamp No. 383. A seven-light pond-lily lamp with drop cluster that originally cost $110 new sold at auction at Parke-Bernet in New York in January 1971 for $1,900. In April 1971, also at Parke-Bernet, a lamp with a mushroom base No. 337 and a heavy rib shade No. 1424 (see Appendix 2, No. 3) sold for $1,800, and a lamp with a dragonfly shade No. 1462 sold for $2,500. In Chicago in February 1971, a ten-light lily went for $3,750; a floor lamp brought $2,900, and a chandelier 22 inches in diameter sold for $3,100.

196. Oil lamp with turtleback tiles in base and shade. *Tiffany Studios Photo, Tuck Collection.*

195. Base No. 179, shade No. 1473. A note on the back of the photo reads "1899 for Mrs. B. Sterns." *Tiffany Studios Photo, Tuck Collection.*

197. Electric lamp, turtleback base, blown glass shade with prisms. *Tiffany Studios Photo, Tuck Collection.*

199. Dragonfly lamp, base No. 397, shade No. 1507. The prices of $150 and $175 correspond to the Price List of 1906. *Tiffany Studios Photo, Tuck Collection.*

198. Mosaic and turtleback base No. 355, peony shade. The price of $750 written on the photograph seems exaggerated. *Tiffany Studios Photo, Tuck Collection.*

200. Dragonfly lamp, shade No. 1495. *Tiffany Studios Photo, Tuck Collection.*

201. Oil lamps, Greek design, No. 181. *Tiffany Studios Photo, Tuck Collection.*

202. Similar to the lamp in Ill. 201, but not identified. *Tiffany Studios Photo, Tuck Collection.*

203. Electric lamp with seven Favrile glass globes; not identified. *Tiffany Studios Photo, Tuck Collection.*

204. Electric lamp, blown glass base and shade. *Tiffany Studios Photo, Tuck Collection.*

205. Electric "panel" lamp, base No. 434, shade No. 1565. *Tiffany Studios Photo, Tuck Collection.*

206. Electric lamp, bronze and coppered glass, numbers not identified. *Tiffany Studios Photo, Tuck Collection.*

207. Grape design lamp. The tree base was "designed by Louis C. Tiffany," according to Alvin J. Tuck. *Tiffany Studios Photo, Tuck Collection.*

208. Wisteria lamp, list No. 342. *Tiffany Studios Photo, Tuck Collection.*

209. Apple blossom lamp. *Tiffany Studios Photo, Tuck Collection.*

210. Number not identified. *Tiffany Studios Photo, Tuck Collection.*

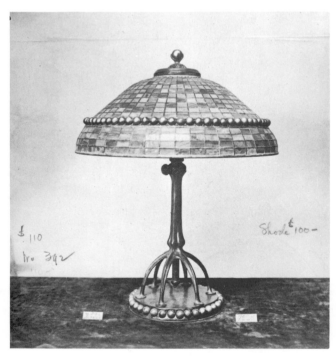

211. Electric lamp base No. 392, shade No. 1508, priced $110 and $100 as in the Price List of 1906. *Tiffany Studios Photo, Tuck Collection.*

212. Lamp base No. 437, shade No. 1485. *Tiffany Studios Photo, Tuck Collection.*

213. Electric lamp base No. 322 with a blown Favrile glass shade. A note indicates that this base was designed by Alvin J. Tuck for Mrs. H. Evans of 20 Fifth Avenue, New York City, and was the first Tuck design to become a stock item at Tiffany Studios. *Tiffany Studios Photo, Tuck Collection.*

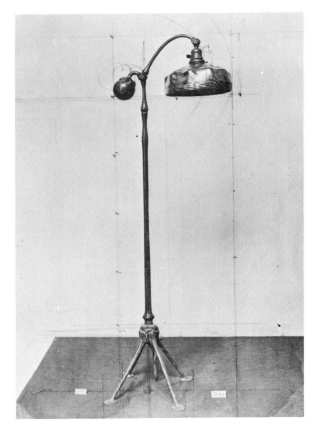

214. Weight-balance lamp No. 414. *Tiffany Studios Photo, Tuck Collection.*

215. Floor lamp No. 471 designed in 1905 by Alvin J. Tuck. *Tiffany Studios Photo, Tuck Collection.*

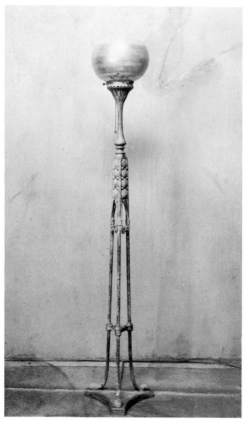

216. Floor lamp No. 378, also designed by Alvin J. Tuck. *Tiffany Studios Photo, Tuck Collection.*

217–236. ALL TIFFANY STUDIOS PHOTOS FROM THE TUCK COLLECTION, WITH THE FOLLOWING NOTES:

Ill. 221: *"Designed for Mr. Biselle"*
Ill. 222: *"List number 380"*
Ill. 223: *"Designed for a Cleveland man"*
Ill. 227: *"Oil lamp for dining room"*
Ill. 235: *"List No. 418, $32."*

218

219

220

221

222

223

224

225

226

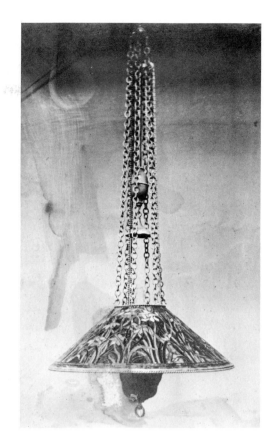

227

228

229

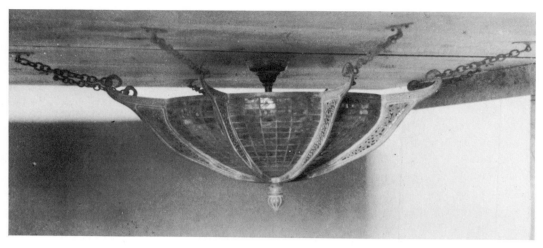

230

231

232

233

235

234

236

237. Electric lamp No. 319 usually referred to as the "three-light lily."

238. All-glass "candle" lamp made in several sizes for candles, oil, or electricity.

239. Tiffany glass jewel shade on No. 533 bronze base. The shade is not signed, as it was not intended to be duplicated or made for retail sale. Author's Collection.

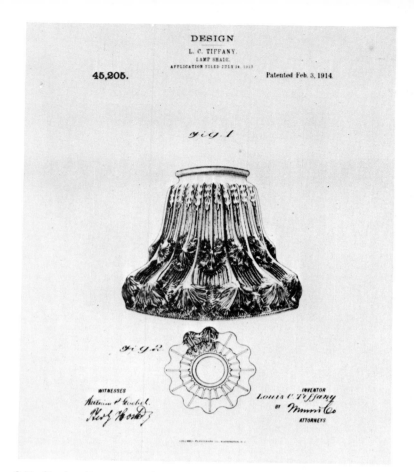

241. Design Patent awarded to Louis C. Tiffany for a glass lampshade Feb. 3, 1914.

240. Lamp with a kapa shell shade, original price $25. *Tiffany Studios Photograph.*

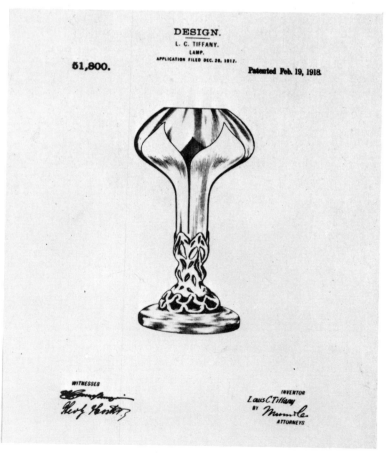

242. Design Patent for a lamp designed by Tiffany in 1918.

243. Impression from a rubber stamp used for designs at Tiffany Studios.

244. Tiffany Studios order form for bronzes, lamps, and other metal products.

Even more spectacular in increased demand and the resulting increase in price are the Tiffany lamps with large, leaded-glass floral shades. Most notable of these has been the Wisteria, No. 342 (Ill. 208), which sold in 1906 for $400. It brought the record price at the Chicago Art Galleries in November 1970 of $18,500.

As scarcity is a factor that influences price, much effort has gone into trying to determine how many of each specific model of lamp were actually produced by Tiffany Studios, but with very little success. Some lamps were unique. The glass jewel shade shown in Ill. 239 has no signature or number, and so it may be a one-of-a-kind item. Oil lamp No. 146, with its floral mosaic base and cobweb shade, is a very desirable lamp. I know of only six. One, made for electricity, No. 1146, is shown as frontispiece. The other five are all in important collections. A lamp of this type has never yet been sold at auction.

Also in the author's collection is a 22-inch dogwood design shade marked "1504-27," which indicates that it is the twenty-seventh shade to be made in that design. Hence, there were at least twenty-six more shades of the same size, shape, and design at one time. However, as these shades were all handmade, no two are ever exactly alike. Also, the craftsmen were often allowed to pick and match their own colors, and so there are often very important variations in the color schemes of the floral shades. Poppies can vary from pale yellow to bright red,

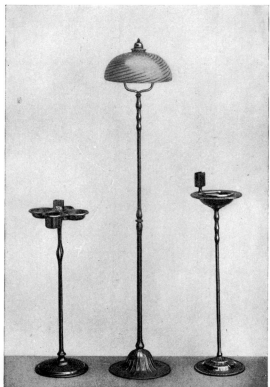

No. 20 Floor Lamp.—Heavy cast bronze, Favrile Glass swing shade. Finished in any standard color.
No. 21 Floor Lamp.—Heavy cast bronze, perforated floral motif. Designed for fabric shade.
M'f'd by L. C. Tiffany Furnaces, Inc., Corona, L. I., N. Y.

No. 19 Floor Lamp.—Heavy cast bronze with Favrile Glass swing shade. Finished in any standard color.
No. 252 Smoker Stand with two receptacles for cigars or cigarettes, two ash trays and match safe. Bronze with enamel inlay.
No. 251 Smoker Stand.—Heavy cast bronze with enamel inlays. Favrile Glass ash tray lining.
M'f'd by L. C. Tiffany Furnaces, Inc., Corona, L. I., N. Y.

245. Two lamps designed and made by Tiffany Furnaces, Inc., between 1919 and 1928.

246. Lamp and two smoker stands, 1919–1928.

peonies from white to red, and roses or tulips can appear in glass of many colors. Preference for colors, again, is often a matter of personal choice, and so the owner of each poppy or peony shade can maintain that his is the best no matter how many others were made from the same pattern.

As the prices of these lamps have risen, some lamps with newly forged signatures have appeared on the market. It is fairly easy to make a little metal tag stamped "Tiffany Studios, New York" in block letters and solder it onto any old or new shade. Unsigned Tiffany-type lamps are far more plentiful and far less expensive than the genuine Tiffanys. Recently I was offered two very fine lamps that I had seen illustrated in a Duffner and Kimberly catalogue. I would have bought them if someone had not added a Tiffany Studios metal label and if they had not been priced at more than they were worth.

Photographs of over 150 lamps are included in this volume, all of which are complete and genuine Tiffany with the proper matching shades and bases. A study of these and a careful examination of a few originals in museums will provide the collector with the knowledge that may prevent him from making mistakes. However, as no book can ever be complete, there always will be the need to consult an expert on some of the more unusual items.

After 1919 Tiffany Studios, under the direction of Joseph Briggs, continued in operation without the benefits of the Tiffany Furnaces. They continued making leaded shades to fit whatever bases were on hand with very few, if any, innovations. I had the pleasure of meeting one of the craftsmen employed by Tiffany Studios as a cutter and maker of leaded shades, but did not succeed in obtaining much reliable information from him or his family. The techniques using copper foil for making leaded or coppered glass shades as practiced at Tiffany's are still known to many craftsmen, and old shades can still be repaired so that they look almost as good as new. The major problem with repairs is matching the old glass. Repairs on lampshades can usually be detected on close examination.

Examples of the products of Tiffany Furnaces managed by A. Douglas Nash can be seen in Ills. 245 and 246. They had to operate without the benefit of the leaded glass made at Tiffany Studios. This necessity led to a rather interesting innovation, probably developed by Patricia Gay, which consisted of lampshades of enamel on a wire mesh. These were occasionally designed with a strong tendency toward Art Deco style. They were not extensively publicized and are not yet as well known or as desirable as the lamps produced by Tiffany in the first two decades of the twentieth century.

NINE

POTTERY, ENAMELS, AND JEWELRY

In 1898 when the Tiffany metal furnaces were established, a department was also created for enameling on metal. However, it was not until 1902, after the death of his father, that Louis C. Tiffany devoted much of his attention to expanding the materials used by Tiffany Studios to include ceramics, enamels, gold, silver, and gemstones. The new line was first exhibited at the Louisiana Purchase Exposition in St. Louis in 1904. There, in the Department of Art, section of Applied Arts, were shown two groups of objects designed by Louis C. Tiffany. The first, lent by Tiffany Furnaces, included forty pieces of Favrile glass, twelve copper vases and bowls enriched with translucent enamels, and three pieces of Favrile pottery. The second group lent by Tiffany and Company will be discussed below.

Tiffany Favrile pottery was made entirely of a white semiporcelain clay, a mixture of clays from Ohio and Massachusetts. It was usually molded rather than wheel-thrown. The term "Favrile" is here used as a trademark rather than meaning "handmade." Nevertheless, Tiffany

247. Tiffany Favrile pottery bowl, scarab decoration in bisque finish.

pottery is of the craftsman variety, carefully finished by hand and glazed in a way consistent with the shape and decoration.

An article by Clara Ruge, published in *The International Studio,* March 1906, under the title "American Ceramics," describes the impression made by the appearance of Tiffany pottery:

Very often the Gruebys have successfully used their vases as lampstands and have combined them with Tiffany's Favrile glass with beautiful effect. But probably Tiffany will in future produce the lamps altogether, because we must welcome as the newest of American potteries the Favrile potteries, executed under the supervision of Louis C. Tiffany in the Tiffany Furnaces at Corona, Long Island. The great facilities of the Tiffany furnaces made it possible to conduct experiments on such a large scale that excellent results could be obtained very promptly. The body used is in porcelain, but for the plastic decorations other clays are employed. The slender forms chosen often approach those of the Favrile glassware. But while the glass shows plant motifs in the forms of objects themselves, in the Tiffany ceramics plastic decorations are used. Water plants, especially the lotos, and the poppy, are employed with great taste, and various kinds of creepers, cereals and the fuchsia.

Antique decorations are chosen occasionally, especially for round pieces. The colour was at first almost exclusively a deep ivory, sometimes shading into brownish effects. Of late, greenish tints have been effectively employed. The large vases are made in beautiful greenish tints, without decorations, but sometimes with a peculiar rough surface, to give certain effects of light and shade. The latest productions, however, have an entirely soft surface. To the mat glaze, crystalline effects are added, and the colouring varies from light to deep green. The vases are of exquisite beauty. The colour effects of the Tiffany Favrile pottery is [*sic*] produced—as in the case of the glass—not through painting on the surface, but by chemical mixtures added to the clays.

248. Tiffany Favrile pottery vase with green glaze, textured rough finish, as pictured in *The International Studio,* December 1906.

Right from the start, Louis C. Tiffany himself took an active interest in the work of his potters. This has been made clear by the late Wilhelm Jenkins who, for five years, was chief muffler in the pottery department at Tiffany Furnaces. Jenkins claimed that some of the first master pots were hand-thrown on the wheel by Mr. Tiffany, and that only Mr. Tiffany could scratch his L C T on the base of a piece of pottery when it was ready for first firing. Shortly before his death, Jenkins explained in detail to a young potter, Peter Rembetsy, the techniques used at Tiffany's to achieve some unusual effects. Some of this information was as follows:

Tiffany pottery was high fire, at approximately 2100 degrees Fahrenheit. A master pot was designed by Mr. Tiffany for each shape and then a mould was made from each master. The number of castings was limited and every piece was hand carved, trimmed and carefully finished before firing. Some of the

249. Ivory Favrile pottery from Tiffany Furnaces, a photograph published in December 1906.

250. Tiffany pottery, mushroom design, brown glaze. Author's Collection.

251. Pair of covered jars, Tiffany pottery, bisque finish.

moulds were simple shapes and the effects of decoration were achieved by the carving.

The greenware, after it had been approved and signed with the L C T monogram, was fired in a large coal-burning kiln and then glazed in the interior with a glaze of blue, green, or brown. The "antique green" glaze was the most frequently used; it matured at 700 degrees Centigrade. This allowed flexibility in the use of other colors in combination with the antique green. For exterior effects, many experiments were made to achieve a good peacock blue "like that of the Sung Dynasty," and a dull gold or bronze effect in brown glaze. Bronze pottery was developed after 1910.

According to Wilhelm Jenkins:

Mr. Tiffany was a nice man but a hard man to work for. One day we were running tests on a batch of glaze, Mr. Tiffany was there—he was always there—when a worker dropped a cigar stub out of his pocket into the vat. I figured to pick it out but Mr. Tiffany raged at the worker and ordered the entire batch destroyed. Many times I saw things like that happen and much money wasted. Normally all waste was conserved. Glass was remelted and used again. Broken

252–253. Assortment of shapes of Tiffany pottery from unsold lot of Tiffany Studios.

pottery was used for experiments. Leftover glazes were used in combination with other glazes for new effects. Supervisors were employed to cut down on waste but quality came first. Mr. Tiffany had to have things exact and was not one to play. He was a hard man to know.

The gold glaze was achieved by a combination of two glazes applied at different temperatures to become laminated:

First an opaque glaze was fused at a high temperature, the pot was removed to the muffle and allowed to cool to 600 degrees C. Then pure gold, in powder form, was mixed with a low fire clear glaze in a proportion that always had to be checked by Mr. Tiffany. This was then sprayed into the muffle, where the heat of the pot would pick it out of the air and cause it to fuse on the surface. This process took approximately 14 hours from start to finish and the temperatures had to be controlled not to vary more than 50 degrees C., a difficult problem in a coal burning kiln.

Only the glazed and finished products were sold at Tiffany and Company. They were advertised as "Tiffany Favrile Pottery, made under the supervision of Mr. Louis C. Tiffany. Artistic effects are produced entirely different from anything heretofore shown, in table

254. Monogram LCT carved into the base of Tiffany Favrile pottery.

lamps, vases, jars and other pieces, now in process of manufacture. Descriptions and prices upon request. $5.00 upward."

However, it was possible to purchase pottery at Tiffany Studios and have it glazed to order. A selection of test tiles was kept on hand there, as well as a variety of shapes of unglazed pottery. The white unglazed pots could be purchased and used as bisque ware, or any pot could be glazed to match a particular tile. This practice continued until at least 1910, when Wilhelm Jenkins was replaced by "a young lady from Scandenavia" who took charge of the glazing of the pottery.

After 1910 it was the bronze pottery that was featured at Tiffany's. This was an all-metal surface applied, instead of a glaze, to the same body and shapes as those made to be glazed. Two methods were used to apply the bronze. One was a sleeve that was caused to shrink around the clay; the other was a form of electroplating. Bronze pottery could then be finished with some of the same formulas for patinas as were applied to metalwares. Relatively few of these bronze pottery pieces were made. In 1946 when the Tiffany personal collection from Laurelton Hall was sold at auction, included in the sale were forty-one pottery tiles, perhaps the samples for glazes, and eighty-seven pottery vases and jars, but only three of these were bronzed. Based on the numbers, the total production of Tiffany pottery made up as vases, bowls, and jars was less than fifteen hundred items made between 1902 and 1914, a much more limited use for pottery than for glass or bronze. Tiffany pottery is very scarce.

Tiffany enamels on copper are also scarce items available only to the most advanced collectors, as their production was even more limited than the production of pottery. The enamel department was launched before 1900, and the results appeared for the first time as color added to the bronze base of the dandelion lamp sent to the Paris World's Fair in 1900 (Ill. 189). In 1902 examples of enamels on repoussé copper forms were illustrated in *The Craftsman,* and a dozen such items were included in the St. Louis Exposition in 1904. In the Tiffany and Company *Blue Book* of 1911 the claim is made that enamels "made under the supervision of Louis C. Tiffany [received] highest awards, Buffalo 1901: Turin 1902." The prices ranged from $10 to $900. Included were small trays, pen trays, vases, and "inkstands of richly carved glass, enamel cover set with opals." The latter sold from $100 to $225. Only large bonbon boxes and vases were more expensive.

Writing in *The Craftsman* in 1902, Samuel Howe explained the process as follows:

The future extensive use of enamel seems to be assured, since experiments are now making, under the direction of Mr. Louis C. Tiffany, in his studio at Corona, Long Island, with the purpose of doing for enamel what has already been accomplished for glass. And surely all that ingenuity, skill and knowledge can suggest, this artist will work out and complete!

Mr. Tiffany is not content with having re-discovered the processes of the glass-workers of Pompeii and Herculaneum, producing by these methods table-vessels and lamps, beautiful in color, well annealed and perfectly made: greatly superior for practical use to the antiques which are sadly lacking in sanitary qualities. He has further applied certain of these secrets to the study of the sister art of enameling: enamels being, as is well known, glass, and glass silicate colored with metallic oxides. His efforts are now centered in the application of enamel to vases ornamented with fruits, flowers, or conventional designs in high relief; his processes being of course unknown outside of his studio, but certain shapes being evidently hammered up from pitch molds, in the usual way, afterward rounded into vase-form, and lastly closed at the bottom.

The desired relief being secured, he adds "paillons," or, as the French word signifies, "spangles," which are small sheets of absolutely pure gold or silver, of from thirty to fifty times the thickness of gold leaf; these are embedded in transparent enamel, or in the surface of the copper foundation, without allowing air to penetrate beneath. Or again, an opaque enamel is floated over the relief ornament: a process difficult even for flat surfaces, and still more complicated when applied to relief ornament. Over this opaque substance, colored enamel is then added according to the design; thin, transparent glazes being mainly used to produce the quality needed. In cases when the natural color of the metal enters into the scheme, the glaze is permitted to over-run the entire subject, giving a still further tone, by increasing depth, perspective and lustre.

Superimposed enamel, that is: the placing of thin layers of transparent substance one over the other, is attended with the danger of chipping, and with great expense,—the latter owing to the number of firings and of annealings necessary, and the risk consequent upon them. But this transparent, or semi-opaque method, notwithstanding its difficulties and its cost, is a real boon to craftsmen, since it affords them a last opportunity to harmonize their strong, crude, and sometimes brutal tones, by removing what is technically known as "the grin," and by softening, enriching and intensifying their effects.

The enamelwork was done entirely by women. Julia Munson was in charge until 1903, when she was transferred to jewelry, and Alice Goovey replaced her. Patricia Gay was also trained at this time, and there were several other apprentices as well. Their production was limited. They never repeated the same color schemes, and their style was distinctive as it was patterned after principles established by Tiffany for all his products.

Most, but not all, Tiffany enamels were signed. Those in Louis C. Tiffany's private collection were marked exactly as was the glass. One in the author's collection reads "L. C. Tiffany 154 A-Coll." Others

255. Tiffany enamel vase of repoussé copper, illustrated in *The Craftsman*, June 1903.

256. Covered box, enamel on copper, with red apples and green leaves. Cutout areas reveal iridescent gold glass; signed on base "Louis C. Tiffany SC309 A Coll." *The Metropolitan Museum of Art, Gift of Louis Comfort Tiffany Foundation, 1951.*

257. Vase, enamel on copper with raised leaves in red and green, is inscribed on the base "L.C.T. EL92." *The Metropolitan Museum of Art, Gift of Louis Comfort Tiffany Foundation, 1951.*

were marked with the initials "L. C. T." or the full name "Louis C. Tiffany," always on the base of the piece. The numbers are often prefixed with the initials "E. L.," "E. G.," or "S. G." No one seems to be sure about the meanings of these letters.

Photographs of examples in the Metropolitan Museum of Art acquired from the Louis Comfort Tiffany Foundation (Ills. 257–259) show some of the shapes characteristic of Tiffany's enamels. Their style is clearly related to that of the glass, bronzes, and lamps from the same factory. Late in 1970 a Tiffany enamel vase, 14½ inches tall, repoussé, with a design of cornstalks, sold at auction in New York for $1,600.

Tiffany Studios also made objects in sterling silver and in both 14- and 18-karat gold. In the Museum of Modern Art, Joseph Heil Collection, there is a Tiffany silver mirror with a peacock enameled on the back, and in the Metropolitan Museum of Art is a three-handled silver cup set with turquoises and emeralds that is clearly marked "Tiffany Studios/New York/Sterling/925/1000/4787" (Ill. 260). The final number, 4787, is yet another puzzle not solved. The use of gold was only recently verified during the cleaning of a small Tiffany Studios seal set with two Favrile glass scarabs—it turned out to be made of solid gold.

Most of the gold and silver work designed by Louis C. Tiffany was made up by Tiffany and Company. In 1902 the son of the founder of Tiffany and Company became the second vice-president and art

258. Bowl, enamel on copper with raised berries in red and green, is inscribed "L.C.T. EL230." *The Metropolitan Museum of Art, Gift of Louis Comfort Tiffany Foundation, 1951.*

259. Vase, enamel on copper with three dragonflies, is inscribed "L.C.T. EL261." *The Metropolitan Museum of Art, Gift of Louis Comfort Tiffany Foundation, 1951.*

260. Three-handled cup, sterling silver set with emeralds and turquoises, is stamped in base "Tiffany Studios, New York, Sterling 95/1000, 4787." *The Metropolitan Museum of Art, Edgar J. Kaufmann Charitable Foundation Fund, 1969.*

director of his father's firm, and he then set up his own separate jewelry department in the Fifth Avenue store. Twenty-five items of jewelry were displayed at the St. Louis World's Fair of 1904 as "designed by Louis C. Tiffany, lent by Tiffany and Company." Some of them were listed as follows:

Tiara of clover leaves and blossoms enamelled on silver; Wild carrot ornament, Enamels with green garnets, opals, diamonds and rubies; Sage ornament, transparent enamel; Nanny berry ornament, white enamel, green cut leaves; Dragon fly ornament, filagree silver and opals; Gold blackberry hair ornament with enamel, garnets, carnelians and coral; Solanum girdle of silver with enamel, Mexican opals and carnelians; Gold necklace, enamel with sapphires and Demantoids.

Similar jewelry designed by Louis C. Tiffany and made at Tiffany and Company in the artistic jewelry department managed by Julia Munson was exhibited at the Paris Salon of 1905 and mentioned in *The International Studio* in December 1906. The 1911 *Blue Book* listed:

Tiffany Art Jewelry. Designed and made under the personal supervision of Mr. Louis C. Tiffany. No pieces duplicated. Among the features of this work are the remarkable color effects obtained in the combinations of gold and enamel with precious and semi-precious stones.

The range of prices was from five dollars for scarf pins to one pendant that listed for $4,875. There were brooches, charms, collars, corsage ornaments, cuff links and pins, earrings, hair ornaments, hat-pins, lorgnons, necklaces, pendants, rings, scarf pins, stoles, and watch chains. They were all marked Tiffany and Company, with no further indication of their special qualities except in the design and workmanship. Five years later, in the *Blue Book* of 1916, a few new items were added to the list, such as bandeaux from $125 to $375; enameled bonbon boxes and vases of gold and silver, some set with precious stones, from $22 to $2,700; bracelets; a dragonfly hair ornament, set with opals, for $300; and a paper cutter of abalone shell, chased gold, and ebony, for $325.

No new items of Tiffany Art Jewelry were made after 1919, the year of the partial retirement of Louis C. Tiffany. The Tiffany Furnaces managed by Douglas Nash between 1919 and 1928 did make some objects of sterling silver decorated with enamels, and these are marked exactly as were the bronzes of this late period of production.

Louis C. Tiffany was seventy years of age when he retired in Jan-

261. Wild carrot and dandelion hair ornaments, designed by Louis C. Tiffany, made by Tiffany and Company, exhibited in St. Louis in 1904, in Paris in 1905, and pictured in *The International Studio* in December 1906.

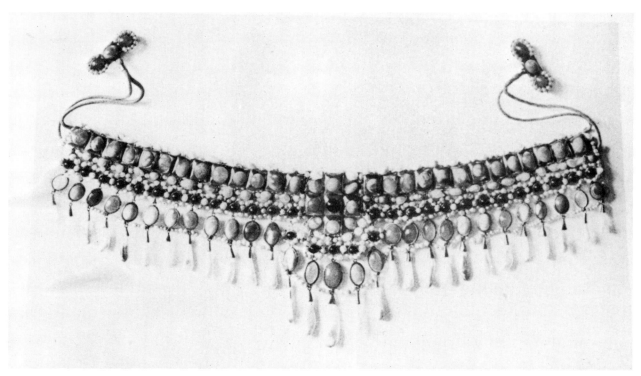

262. "Corsage ornament" of 18-karat gold, opals, and whole pearls designed by Louis C. Tiffany and made by Tiffany and Company in 1904, pictured in *The International Studio*, 1906.

263. Necklace of 14-karat gold, amethysts, and jade, designed by Louis C. Tiffany and made by Tiffany and Company in 1904, pictured in *The International Studio*, 1906.

264. Hair ornament of silver flowers with stamens of gold; sterling silver wire frame for Favrile glass bowl; deadly nightshade pendant, all designed by Louis C. Tiffany, pictured in *The International Studio,* 1906.

265. Solanum girdle made of sterling silver berries, enameled silver, carnelians, and Mexican opals, designed by Louis C. Tiffany, pictured in *The International Studio,* 1906.

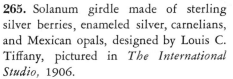

uary of 1919. From then until his death in 1933 he continued painting, mostly in oils, and devoted much time to the establishment of
the Louis Comfort Tiffany Foundation. He was well aware of the
future potential of his products, as he is reputed to have said, "Some-
day people will make a lot of money from the things I will leave behind." His prophecy would have been realized sooner if it had not
been for the Depression of the thirties and the war in the forties. And,
also, the taste for purist "functionalism" in architecture and interior
design created a generally negative approach to naturalistic ornament
in the second quarter of the twentieth century.

The myth that much of Tiffany's work was destroyed appears to be
grossly exaggerated. Certainly some of the glass was broken, either from
carelessness or neglect; some bronzes were donated as scrap to help the
war effort during World War II, and some lamps were discarded as
junk. I purchased my first Tiffany bronze lamp with a leaded glass
shade in 1955 for $25 and several Tiffany bronze candlesticks for two
dollars each. Then nobody cared whether or not they were genuine
signed Tiffany. Most of that which was lost consisted of the cheaper
imitations that were made in much greater quantities.

As already stated, it has been impossible to determine exactly how
many bronzes or lamps were made in Tiffany Furnaces from 1898
until 1918. They keep turning up, and there is a steady increase in

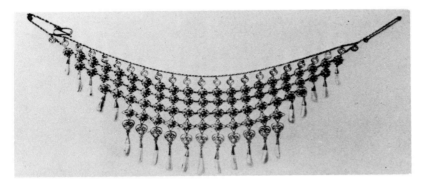

266. Necklace of 14-karat gold set with pearls, designed by Louis C.
Tiffany, pictured in *The International Studio,* 1906.

267. Watercolor design for a lamp, signed by Louis C. Tiffany. *The Metropolitan Museum of Art, Gift of Walter Hoving, 1967.*

HANGING · DOME · SHADE

· MR · J · R · MARTIN ·
· BELLEVUE · PALACE ·
· BERN · SWITZERLAND ·

APPROVED

Louis C. Tiffany

268. Watercolor design for a hanging dome lamp for a palace in Switzerland, approved and signed by Louis C. Tiffany. *The Metropolitan Museum of Art, Gift of Julia Weld, 1967.*

their price as the number of collectors constantly grows. It is a free market, with prices depending on supply and demand. Even though the figures are not known, the supply is a fixed one whose availability can only decrease while the demand increases, as it continues to do. It is therefore probable that the prices of Tiffany's products will continue to rise, no matter how high they may already be in today's marketplace. The collector must depend on information, such as is contained in this volume, to determine authenticity. Beyond that, collecting is largely a matter of taste. The only reason Tiffany floral lamps are more expensive than Tiffany geometrics is that they are more decorative, more publicized, and therefore more in demand.

APPENDIX 1

PRICE LIST *

October 1, 1906

These Prices Provide for Any Finish Except for
Lamps. 20% Additional for Silver; 25% Additional
for Gold, on All Lamps

---

* According to Donald T. Buck, Assistant Professor of Economics at Southern
Connecticut State College, in 1906 the average hourly wage in manufacturing and certain nonmanufacturing jobs was 17½ cents. In 1970 the average was $3.29. Thus, the
average hourly wage rate might be interpreted as having increased 18½ times by 1970.
Further research seems to imply that the prices of household goods increased roughly 5½
times during that same period. These figures should be helpful in interpreting the prices
in this list in the light of today's values. Where no price is given for an item in the
Tiffany Price List reproduced here, none appeared in the original.

OIL LAMPS *

*Patent
No.*
                                                                          Price

101. Single student, wire decoration, Gothic-Mammoth . . $40.00
102. Single student, wire decoration, Tiffany-Mammoth . .   40.00
103. Single student, wire decoration, elliptical-Mammoth .   40.00
104. Single student, wire decoration, rope-Mammoth . .   40.00
105. Single student, wire decoration, diamond-Mammoth .   40.00
108. Single student, small cylindrical, Tiffany design, No. 1   28.00
109. Single student, small cylindrical, double triangle, de-
        sign No. 1 . . . .   28.00
112. Single student, small urn font, lattice design, No. 18 .   35.00
113. Single student, small urn font, plain design, No. 18 .   18.00
114. Single student, small cylindrical, plain, No. 1 . . .   10.00
115. Single student, plain, Mammoth 18.00
116. Single student, duplex burner, acorn, rope design . .   40.00
119. Double student, duplex burner, acorn, rope design . .   50.00
120. Double student, plain, Mammoth 35.00
121. Double student, plain, small urn font 25.00
122. Double student, plain, Hartshorn shape 50.00
123. Double student, globe font, perforated elaborate . .   150.00
124. Double student, etched Hartshorn 55.00
125. Double student, Repousse-Hartshorn 150.00
126. Double student, Flame-Hartshorn 70.00
127. Double student, Japanese-Hartshorn 60.00
129. Double student, Honeycomb-Hartshorn 60.00
130. Double student, wire decoration, Gothic, Mammoth .   50.00
131. Double student, wire decoration, Tiffany, Mammoth .   50.00

---

* B.G. means Blown Glass
  F.G. means Favrile Glass
  T.B. means Turtle Backs
  E.M. & G. means Etched Metal and Glass
  W.C. means Wild Carrot

132.	Double student, wire decoration, rope, Mammoth . .	50.00
133.	Double student, wire decoration, elliptical, Mammoth	50.00
134.	Double student, wire decoration, spiral, Mammoth .	50.00
136.	Double student, small urn font, wire and bead . . .	40.00
137.	Double student, wire decoration, Diamond, Mammoth	50.00
138.	Double student, small urn, eclipse and lattice . . .	40.00
139.	FLOWER POT, saucer, base	35.00
141.	WILD CARROT cast (shade for same $50) . . .	65.00
142.	NIGHT BLOOMING CEREUS, cast	75.00
144.	Simple Indian design-cast	60.00
145.	Mosaic arrowhead-squat	75.00
146.	Mosaic floral base, cobweb shade	500.00
147.	Mosaic DRAGONFLY	100.00
148.	Mosaic primrose base, butterfly shade	500.00
149.	Mosaic plain squares, squat 11″ diameter	100.00
150.	Mosaic, same as No. 148, but metal base	350.00
151.	Mosaic wheat base, cobweb and apple blossom shade	200.00
152.	Spun font, not separate, wire decoration, bowl shape .	25.00
153.	Spun font, not separate, etched, bowl shape	18.00
154.	Spun font, not separate, wire, bowl like No. 156. .	25.00
155.	Spun font, not separate, etched, bowl like No. 156. .	18.00
156.	Spun font, not separate, plain	15.00
157.	Spun font, not separate, plain	15.00
158.	Spun font, separate	15.00
159.	Spun font, not separate	15.00
160.	Spun urn, like No. 161, chased lines	25.00
161.	Spun, squat urn, plain	20.00
162.	Spun, wave design	30.00
163.	Spun, round-long arms from body, light chasing . .	35.00
164.	Spun, tall, egg shape, plain	30.00
165.	Spun, squat-flare base	18.00
166.	Spun, gourd, low	18.00
167.	Spun, pear shape, plain	25.00
168.	Spun, pear shape, pin needle decorations	30.00
169.	Spun, like No. 166, Japanese decoration	25.00
170.	Spun, like No. 166, etched band	20.00
171.	Spun, like No. 165, tobacco leaf decoration . . .	25.00
172.	Spun, egg shape, etched band	33.00
173.	Spun, gourd in tripod stand, chased lines	25.00
174.	Spun, gourd in tripod stand, etched band	25.00
175.	Gourd in tripod stand, metal deposit	25.00

177. Spun oval lamp, three-leaf turtle back ornament, cast base 45.00
178. Tripod oil lamp, tall 75.00
179. Tyler, trumpet shape, pod design 75.00
180. Crutch oval lamp, T.B. band, elec. No. 446 . . . . 40.00
181. Greek design, large 30.00
182. Greek design, small 25.00
183. Greek design, large F.G. body 40.00
184. Greek design, small F.G. body 30.00
185. Spun urn shape cradle 35.00
186. Leaf base 30.00
187. Three stem 40.00
188. Spun torpedo cradle 30.00
189. Spun oval body, swamp flower base 30.00
190. Claw foot, 3 legs, flat round base 30.00
191. B.G. in metal, oval, Persian design 65.00
192. B.G. in metal, oval, 3 leaf design 65.00
193. B.G. in metal, oval, shell design, metal deposit, etched 65.00
194. B.G. in metal, star-fish design 65.00
195. Claw foot, 3 legs, flat-round base, small like No. 190 25.00
198. CORINTHIAN COLUMN 35.00
199. DORIC COLUMN 30.00
201. PUMPKIN, Pond Lily base 60.00
203. Tyler, trumpet shape, plain 60.00
210. Plain PUMPKIN 20.00
211. Pony PUMPKIN, F.G. Irid. with globe 30.00
214. PUMPKIN, pebble decoration, with 16″ pebble shade (No. 175) 75.00
215. PUMPKIN, fancy, with Gleason shade, ball fringe . . 100.00
217. Pepper, blown glass, in metal, Pond Lily base . . . 100.00
218. Pepper, all metal leaf base 50.00
219. Pepper, blown glass, in metal—leaf base 100.00
220. Web foot lamp, tear decoration 35.00
221. Saucer base, oval repousse decoration 35.00
222. Saucer base, oval etched band 25.00
223. Web foot, etched fern decorations 30.00
224. PEACOCK, large 115.00
225. CAT-TAIL, Pond Lily base 115.00
226. PEACOCK, glass in body, large, like No. 224 . . . 100.00
227. Square T.B. sides 65.00
230. Piano, floor, extension, elaborate 200.00

258. Cushion base, rising sun design 65.00
289. Blown glass in wire, crab base 115.00
292. B.G. in wire, low large lobes, wire and bead decora-
      tions 100.00

ELECTRIC LAMPS

300. Standard, 3 lights, suspended shade-slide $25.00
301. Standard, 3 lights, upright blossom-slide 35.00
302. Standard, 6 lights, drop blossom-slide 50.00
303. Standard, single swing arm, small slide 27.00
304. Standard, double swing arm, small slide 35.00
305. Standard, 3 lights, drop blossom, plain-slide 25.00
306. Standard, 3 lights, drop blossom on one side-chased-
      slide 25.00
307. Standard, 3 lights, drop blossom, spread-chased-slide   30.00
308. Standard, single swing arm, large-chased-slide . . .   40.00
309. Standard, 3 lights, ribbed stem, chased base-lights
      turned down 40.00
310. Standard, 3 lights, ribbed stem, chased base-lights
      turned up 40.00
311. Standard, 7 lights, upright blossoms, ribbed 60.00
312. Standard, 1 light, student, twist stem 50.00
313. Standard, 4 lights, twist stem, 1 up and 3 drop . . .   45.00
314. Standard, 4 lights, Newel-twist stem, 1 up and 3 drop   75.00
315. Standard, 4 lights, Newel-stiff stem, 1 up and 3 drop   90.00
316. Standard, double swing arm, large 60.00
317. Standard, 3 lights, suspended shades, elaborate . . .   30.00
318. Standard, double swing arm, large, like No. 316, takes
      No. 1410 shade 60.00
319. Standard, 3 lights, drop blossoms, twist, small . . .   25.00
320. Desk, 3 lights, drop blossoms, small 19.00
322. Standard, simple conv. design, small 20.00
323. Standard, crutch slide, small, 3 legs, round base . .   16.00
324. Standard, jeweled base, small 25.00
325. Standard, wild carrot base 15.00
326. Standard, cushion base, ribbed, small 20.00
327. Standard, reed stem, small 20.00
328. Standard, reed stem, large 20.00
329. SEARCHLIGHT lamp, turtle back glass 70.00

330.	DIVERS' LANTERN, portable, turtle back glass . .	60.00
331.	Desk lamp, light below base	30.00
333.	Standard-Lummis, broad ribs	30.00
334.	Desk lamp, curved arm, chased	20.00
335.	Desk lamp, small Greek, like No. 182	25.00
336.	Leaf base, like No. 186	30.00
337.	MUSHROOM, standard, small	90.00
338.	B.G. in metal, PINEAPPLE, 4 leaf legs	80.00
339.	Standard, 3 lights, twist stem, Wilson	30.00
340.	Standard, 4 lights, twist stem, Holden	50.00
341.	WAVE and FISH lamp, cast metal	150.00
342.	WISTARIA lamp and shade, large	400.00
343.	MUSHROOM F.G.	20.00
344.	POND LILY lamp and shade, large	400.00
345.	POND LILY lamp and shade, small	200.00
346.	TRUMPET CREEPER and shade, No. 342 block . .	375.00
347.	APPLE BLOSSOM and shade, No. 342 block . . .	375.00
348.	GRAPE and shade, No. 342 block	375.00
349.	Pony WISTARIA	200.00
350.	Pony BEGONIA	175.00
351.	APPLE BLOSSOM stand and shade, large	425.00
352.	LOTUS lamp and shade, 12 lights, 8 F.G. globes . .	750.00
353.	BAT lamp and shade, complete	125.00
354.	SQUASH, 6 lights, electric lamp and shade, 6 F.G. squash blossom globes	
355.	Mosaic and turtle back lamp, large lights inside . . .	300.00
356.	DRAGONFLY, standard, mosaic and metal, small . .	100.00
357.	Library, standard, cushion base, leaf design	65.00
358.	Library, standard, cushion base, rising sun design . .	65.00
359.	Library, standard, cushion base, tear design	65.00
360.	Library, standard, cushion base, conventional design .	70.00
362.	Library, standard, cushion base, ribbed design . . .	65.00
363.	Library, standard, cushion base, pod design	65.00
364.	Library, standard, cushion base, hammered design . .	65.00
365.	Library, standard, cushion base, mud turtle design . .	65.00
366.	Library, standard, cushion base, large, conventional design, pineapple	90.00
367.	Library, standard, cushion base, large, O'Brien . . .	125.00
368.	Library, standard, cushion base, large Tyler	75.00
369.	Standard, fern design	60.00
370.	Library, standard, mushroom design	50.00

371. Library, standard, Indian Hookah, shade No. 1486 . .   85.00
372. Library, standard, B.G. in metal 80.00
373. Library, standard, mushroom, 6-8 c.p. lights, shade
        No. 1524 . . . .   50.00
374. Library, standard, Dodge, 6-8 c.p. lights, shade No.
        1520 . . . .   75.00
375. Piano, floor, large, wire decoration, scroll 165.00
376. Piano, floor, large, chased pod 165.00
377. Piano, floor, large, plain 115.00
378. Piano, floor, tripod, Vinson 100.00
379. Piano, floor, small, chased pod, Holden 125.00
380. 16 lights, upright, long stem flower lamp, glass extra   125.00
381. 10 lights, drop cluster, pond lily 90.00
382. 12 lights, drop cluster, pond lily 100.00
383. 18 lights, drop cluster, pond lily 125.00
384. Pony APPLE BLOSSOM lamp and shade 200.00
385. 7 lights, drop cluster, pond lily 80.00
386. Piano, floor, tripod, Vinson swing top for 10" shade .   125.00
387. Piano, floor, small, plain, Holden 75.00
388. Piano, floor, No. 230 oil converted 200.00
389. Piano, floor, ring base, 5 heavy rods for stem-slide . .   110.00
390. Standard, 3 lights, 4 legs, 16 prongs, F.G. ball on
        each-slide 110.00
391. 6 lights, standard, 4-legged claw feet-slide 100.00
392. 6 lights, standard, F.G. around base-slide 110.00
393. 6 lights, standard, like No. 425, large-slide 50.00
394. Library, standard, mushroom, new style, like No. 370   50.00
395. Library, standard, similar to No. 363, taller, suspended
        shade 65.00
396. Library, standard, simple, plain stem, 4 legs, inverted
        cradle 20.00
397. Library, standard, 6 lights, cast stem, large-slide . . .   150.00
398. B.G. in wire, crab base, like No. 289 oil 125.00
399. Library standard, 4 light, 4 legs, slide F.G. balls in
        base and stem 110.00
400. Nautilus, leaded glass, chased, shell design 70.00
401. Nautilus, leaded glass, leaf design 60.00
402. Nautilus, natural shell, jeweled base 60.00
403. Nautilus, natural shell, ribbed or chased design . . .   35.00
404. Nautilus, natural shell, mermaid 125.00
405. Nautilus, natural shell, chased shell design 55.00

406.	Nautilus, natural shell, ribbed base, swivel	45.00
408.	Seal lamp, turtle back	55.00
409.	Nautilus, natural shell, chased, leaf design	45.00
410.	Balance lamp, ring and ball, No. 403 base for 7″ shade	35.00
411.	Balance lamp, like No. 414, but smaller T.B.B. weight	40.00
412.	Scarab, small	30.00
413.	Balance lamp and shade, B.G. in metal	60.00
414.	Balance lamp, Tyler base, well sweep, turtle back weight	80.00
415.	Balance lamp for 10″ shade	35.00
416.	Balance lamp, "Claflin"	30.00
417.	Balance lamp, well sweep	30.00
418.	Bell lamp for 7″ shade, low, pivot	20.00
419.	Bell lamp, for 7″ shade, high, ribbed, pivot	23.00
420.	Bell lamp, for globe, large	20.00
421.	Bell lamp, for globe, small	20.00
422.	Bell lamp and lotus shade, large, complete	90.00
423.	Bell lamp, for floor, 3 legs, for 10″ shade	45.00
424.	Bell lamp, like No. 419 but taller	25.00
425.	Root base, 3 legs, 2 prongs on each, slide	15.00
426.	Round base, 3-leaf ornament, 3 supports for shade . .	18.00
427.	1 light electric lamp, like No. 1201 candlestick slide .	20.00
428.	1 light electric lamp, like No. 1205 candlestick, bamboo	18.00
429.	1 light electric lamp, hospital lamp, adjustable, shade silk	25.00
430.	1 light floor lamp, searchlight top, turtle back glass .	100.00
431.	1 light, small torpedo bottle holder base	25.00
432.	1 light, root base, 5 legs, 3 prongs on each applied ornament on stem	30.00
433.	1 light, tripod, same as No. 1211 candlestick	22.00
434.	1 light, 4 legs, turtle back glass in base, slide . . .	26.00
435.	1 light, like No. 1215 candlestick, jewel top	28.00
435A.	1 light, tall, like No. 1215 candlestick, jewel top, for 1485 shade	35.00
436.	1 light, plain, square base ring holder, 7″ shade . . .	20.00
437.	See 435A	
438.	Tyler stem, standard, for No. 1546 ball	55.00
438A.	Tyler, stem, 6-8 c.p. lamps, 1524 shade	75.00
438B.	Similar to Tyler ball, 6-lb. reg. sockets for globe . .	80.00
439.	Tripod standard, tall	75.00

440.	4-legged slide, standard, claw feet, Villard	45.00
441.	Greek, narrow	25.00
442.	Bird skeleton, standard	90.00
443.	WATER LILY, standard, twisted stem, No. 1502 shade	65.00
444.	Crutch, long body, square base	30.00
445.	4-play ruffle base, three supports for shade	23.00
446.	Crutch oval lamp, T.B. band, like No. 180	50.00
447.	Plain spun base, tripod holder, special	25.00
448.	1 light, 2 posts, swing top, tall, for bell-shaped F.G. shade	45.00
449.	1 light, 2 posts, swing top, short, for bell-shaped F.G. shade	40.00
452.	3 lights, standard, open-work, wire and ball design, slide	50.00
453.	Cattail, pond lily base, electric	100.00
454.	1 light piano lamp, long swing arm, T.B. base . . .	80.00
457.	Tall, egg-shaped, etched, like No. 172 oil	35.00
458.	Cradle torpedo, like No. 188	35.00
459.	Claw foot, like No. 190	35.00
460.	Three stems, like No. 187 oil	40.00
461.	1 light electric, standard, 4-prong shade holder, Penguin design	
462.	1 light electric, standard, small, like No. 195 lamp . .	
464.	1 light electric, standard, No. 470 base, revolving reflector top, long glass, Osborne	65.00
466.	Floor lamp, No. 423 stem, No. 415 top	65.00
467.	Floor lamp, "Vinson," standard, 3 lights, slide through top of shade	110.00
468.	Balance lamp for floor, No. 423 stem with No. 417 top	55.00
469.	Floor lamp, 4 feet revolving top, lined with opal glass	75.00
470.	Bell lamp for 10″ shade, 8 feet, pivot slide	40.00
471.	Balance lamp for floor, No. 415 top, 4 legs, for 10″ shade	65.00
472.	Piano lamp, large, floor, bamboo design	150.00
473.	Piano lamp, small, floor, bamboo design	125.00
474.	Library lamp, bamboo design, O'Brien size	125.00
475.	See 438A	
476.	Searchlight, No. 470 base, pressed jewel top	80.00
477.	See 438B	
478.	4-legged claw feet slide, with harp top for 10″ F.G. shade	70.00

480. 3 lights, bamboo design, library stand size 65.00
481. 3 lights, 4-legged, claw-foot, library stand size, like
     No. 1201 candlestick 65.00
482. 3 lights, drill design, library stand, like No. 1202
     candlestick . . . .
485. 1 light, like No. 1210 candlestick 25.00
486. 1 light, like No. 1215B candlestick, 10″ tripod holder .   22.00
487. 1 light, like No. 1202 candlestick, regular socket, slide   18.00
490. 4 lights, electric candelabra, 2-2 lt. arms, flame decor   60.00
491. 6 lights, electric candelabra, 3-2 lt. arms, flame decor   75.00
492. 5 lights, electric candelabra, 2-2 lt. arms, one in centre,
     flame decor 67.00
493. 2 lights, electric, like No. 1230B, candlestick 30.00
495. 6 lights, electric, like No. 1290B candlestick 60.00
496. 6 lights, electric, like No. 1291A candlestick 50.00

HANGING SHADES

600. 25″ DOGWOOD, straight sides, circular   Complete $140.00
601. 28″ ALAMANDA, straight sides, circular .   "   165.00
602. 28″ NASTURTIUM and LATTICE, straight
     sides, Circular . . . .   "   160.00
603. 28″ PEONY, straight sides, circular . . .   "   175.00
604. 28″ CLEMATIS, straight sides, circular . .   "   150.00
605. 28″ DOGWOOD, straight sides, circular .   "   150.00
606. 25″ TRUMPET CREEPER, straight sides,
     circular . . . .   "   150.00
607. 25″ NASTURTIUM and LATTICE, straight
     sides, octagon . . . .   "   160.00
608. 28″ GRAPE, straight side, circular . . .   "   160.00
609. 28″ WOODBINE, straight sides, octagon .   "   150.00
610. 28″ NASTURTIUM, no lattice, straight
     sides circular . . . .   "   150.00
611. 30″ GRAPE, 12 sides . . . .   "   200.00
612. 28″ CLEMATIS, straight sides, octagon . .   "   175.00
613. 28″ DRAGON FLY, flying down, straight
     side, circular . . . .   "   175.00
614. 28″ BLACK-EYED SUSAN, straight side,
     circular . . . .   "   175.00
615. 28″ DAFFODIL, straight side, circular . .   "   175.00

616.	28" DRAGON FLY, flying round, straight side, circular	"	175.00
617.	28" SNOWBALL, straight side, circular . .	"	175.00

FANCY GOODS

800.	BOX, E.M. & G., 4½ × 3¼ × 1½	$6.00
801.	BOX, E.M. & G., Stamps	6.00
802.	BOX, Metal, Stamps, Zodiac	6.00
803.	BOX, Metal and Glass, Stamps, Byzantine	25.00
804.	BOX, Metal, Stamps, Book Mark	14.00
805.	BOX, Mosaic, Stamps, double Scarab lid	40.00
806.	BOX, Metal and Glass, Byzantine, 4½ × 3"	
808.	BOX, E.M. & G., 5 × 3¼ × 1¾	8.00
809.	BOX, E.M. & G., 6¾ × 4½ × 2"	10.00
810.	BOX, Metal Zodiac, 5½ × 4½	8.00
811.	BOX, Metal Zodiac, 6½ × 2¾	10.00
812.	BOX, Metal Book Mark for rubber bands	16.00
813.	BOX, E.M. & Glass, cigarette, unlined, 6¾ × 4¼ × 3"	12.00
815.	BOX, E.M. & Glass, cigarette, cedar lined, 6¾ × 4¼ × 3"	14.00
816.	BOX, E.M. & Glass, trays for jewels, plush, 6¾ × 4¼ × 3"	16.00
817.	BOX, Metal, T.B. Glass, casket for jewels	
821.	BOX, E.M. & Glass, handkerchief (small) 7 × 7 × 2½"	15.00
823.	BOX, E.M. & Glass, cigar, cedar lined, water sponge box	25.00
824.	BOX, E.M. & Glass, handkerchief (large) 8 × 8 × 2¾"	16.00
825.	BOX, E.M. & Glass, cigar, unlined, 9 × 6½ × 3" . .	20.00
826.	BOX, E.M. & Glass, cedar lined, 9 × 6½ × 3" . . .	23.00
827.	BOX, E.M. & Glass, gloves, 13½ × 4½ × 3¼" . . .	23.00
828.	BOX, Metal, cigar, cedar lined, shell and barnacles design	30.00
829.	BOX, E.M. & Glass, writing set	40.00
830.	BOX, E.M. & Glass, trays for jewels, 9 × 6½ × 3" . .	30.00
831.	BOX, F.G. Panels & jewels, trays for jewels	
833.	FERN DISH, E.M. & Glass Jardiniere	40.00
834.	FERN DISH, Metal, Marsh Marigold	40.00
835.	FERN DISH, Metal and Mosaic Arrowheads . . .	90.00

836.	FERN DISH, T.B.	45.00
837.	POWDER BOX, Milkweed design, silver	35.00
838.	TWINE BALL HOLDER, E.M. & Glass, hexagon	12.00
839.	POWDER BOX, E.M. & Glass, round	12.00
840.	PASTE POT, E.M. & Glass, with Carter's paste	20.00
841.	POWDER BOX, Japanese, 3¾ × 3"	15.00
842.	INKSTAND, Metal Zodiac, octagonal	12.00
843.	INKSTAND, Metal and Glass, Byzantine	55.00
844.	INKSTAND, E.M. & G., square, large, 3¾ × 3¾ × 3"	15.00
845.	INKSTAND, E.M. & G., square, small, 3 × 3 × 2½"	10.00
846.	INKSTAND, E.M. & G., round, small, 3¾ × 2"	12.00
847.	INKSTAND, E.M. & G., ROUND, large, bent glass, 7"	20.00
848.	INKSTAND, Blown Glass in wire, round, large, diam. 9"	30.00
849.	INKSTAND, Blown Glass in metal, round, large, diam. 7"	35.00
850.	INKSTAND, Blown Glass in metal, conical, diam. 4¼"	20.00
851.	INKSTAND, E.M. & Glass, 2 wells	15.00
852.	INKSTAND, Metal Butterfly, poppy well	18.00
853.	INKSTAND, Marble and Glass Mosaic squares	7.00
854.	INKSTAND, Marble and Glass, Mosaic, round	7.00
855.	INKSTAND, Metal, Wild Carrot, diam. 5½"	12.00
856.	INKSTAND, Metal, Crab	25.00
857.	INKSTAND, Metal, 3 Scarabs	25.00
858.	INKSTAND, Metal, Woven Basket	25.00
859.	INKSTAND, Metal, Japanese	15.00
860.	INKSTAND, Metal Tear	20.00
861.	INKSTAND and PEN TRAY combined, F.G. well	12.00
862.	INKSTAND, Metal, shape No. 860, inlaid, Metal	20.00
863.	INKSTAND, F.G. Metal Top	20.00
864.	INKSTAND, Book Mark	22.00
865.	INKSTAND, Mosaic, round, plain, diam. 4¾"	15.00
866.	INKSTAND, Single Scarab, glass wings	8.00
867.	INKSTAND, Mosaic and Metal, Poppy, diam. 3¾"	30.00
868.	INKSTAND, Mosaic and Metal, swirl 2" high	8.00
869.	INKSTAND, Metal, shape No. 860, metal deposit	20.00
870.	LETTER SCALE, Metal and Glass, Byzantine	25.00
871.	VINGRETTE [*sic*], F.G. Metal Mounts	
872.	LETTER SCALES, E.M. & Glass, small	7.00

874.	LETTER SCALES, Metal Zodiac, small	7.00
875.	CARD CASE, E.M. & G., single	6.00
876.	CARD CASE, E.M. & Glass, double	8.00
877.	CLOCK, E.M. & Glass, small, tower, case, American movement	20.00
880.	LETTER SCALE, Book Mark	
882.	CARD CASE, Book Mark	18.00
889.	TABLE, fluted metal legs, wood top, 14″ square . .	40.00
890.	TABLE, Louis XV style, wood top, 14½″, square . .	125.00
894.	MIRROR, three-fold, Metal and inlaid Glass, 11½″ square	150.00
895.	MIRROR, Hand, E.M. & leather, round	25.00
896.	MIRROR, Table, circular, Peacock, small	75.00
897.	MIRROR, Table, oval, Peacock	100.00
898.	MIRROR, Table, circular, Peacock, large, 15″ . . .	90.00
899.	MIRROR, Table, oval, Pond Lily	115.00
900.	MIRROR, Table, Fern	100.00
902.	MIRROR, Hand, E.M. & Leather, painted, oval . .	35.00
903.	READING GLASS, E.M. & Glass, 3½″ lens	7.00
904.	TEA SCREENS, E.M. & Glass, three-fold, 7¼ × 4″ .	15.00
905.	TWINE HOLDER, Book Mark	
907.	TRAY, E.M. & Glass, Vawter, 15 × 10″	15.00
910.	TEA SCREEN, Plain glass, three-fold, 7¼ × 4″ . . .	9.00
911.	TEA SCREEN, E.M. & Glass	15.00
915.	LEADED TEA SCREEN, Misc., three-fold	30.00
924.	LAMP SCREEN, Butterfly shape	12.00
925.	LAMP SCREEN, Dragonfly shape	12.00
930.	PAPER-WEIGHT, and CALENDAR	4.00
931.	PAPER-WEIGHT, M. & Glass, scroll	5.00
932.	PAPER-WEIGHT, M. & Glass, swirl	8.00
933.	PAPER-WEIGHT, M. & Glass, wave	
934.	PAPER-WEIGHT, Metal Zodiac	3.00
935.	PAPER-WEIGHT, T.B.	7.00
936.	PAPER-WEIGHT, E.M. & Glass, round	4.00
937.	PAPER-WEIGHT, Book Mark	
938.	PAPER-WEIGHT, Crab	20.00
939.	CALENDAR, E.M. & Glass, 7 × 9″, large	12.00
940.	CALENDAR, E.M. & Glass, small 4¼ × 6¼″ . . .	10.00
941.	CALENDAR, E.M. & Glass, miniature, 6⅛ × 4½″ . .	8.00
943.	CALENDAR, Metal, Signs of Zodiac	12.00

944. CALENDAR, Metal & Glass, Byzantine 45.00
945. CALENDAR, Metal, Book Mark 17.00
946. PHOTOGRAPH FRAME, E.M. & Glass, cabinet, oval
     opening 12.00
947. PHOTOGRAPH FRAME, E.M. & Glass, cabinet, ob-
     long 12.00
948. PHOTOGRAPH FRAME, E.M. & Glass, small, 6 ×
     7" 7.00
949. PHOTOGRAPH FRAME, E.M. & Glass, oval open-
     ing 6 × 7", small 7.00
950. PHOTOGRAPH FRAME, 3 fold-cabinet, oblong,
     E.M. & G. 35.00
951. PHOTOGRAPH FRAME, double-cabinet, oblong,
     E.M. & G. 24.00
952. PHOTOGRAPH FRAME, 3 fold-cabinet, oval, E.M.
     & G. 35.00
953. PHOTOGRAPH FRAME, double-cabinet, small, oval,
     E.M. & G. 15.00
954. PHOTOGRAPH FRAME, double E.M. & G., cabinet,
     oval 24.00
955. PHOTOGRAPH FRAME, double E.M., small, oblong   15.00
956. MATCH SAFE, Mosaic, plain, diam. 2¾" 10.00
957. MATCH SAFE, Mosaic, plain, diam. 4¼" 20.00
958. MATCH SAFE, E.M. & G., stand 8.00
959. MATCH SAFE, E.M. & G, no stand 5.00
960. BILL FILE, Marble and Glass, Mosaic, square . . .   15.00
961. BILL FILE, E.M. & Glass, round 4.00
962. BILL FILE, Metal Zodiac 4.00
963. BILL FILE, Metal and Glass, Byzantine 12.00
964. MUCILAGE Pot, E.M. 4.00
965. MATCH SAFE AND ASH TRAY, E.M. & Glass . .   10.00
966. BILL FILE, Book Mark . . . .
967. MUCILAGE POT, Book Mark . . . .
968. PAPER KNIFE, E.M., simple 1.00
969. PAPER KNIFE, E.M. & Glass 4.00
971. LETTER CLIPS, E.M. & Glass 4.00
972. TEA STAND, Mosaic, round, fancy 20.00
973. PEN BRUSH, Book Mark 9.00
974. TEA STAND, Mosaic, round, geometrical 20.00
975. ASH TRAY, Book Mark 7.00

976.	ASH TRAY, Metal Zodiac	3.00
977.	ASH TRAY, E.M. & Glass, 4½ × 3″	4.00
978.	PIN TRAY, E.M. & Glass, 4½ × 3″	4.00
979.	ASH TRAY, Metal and Glass, Byzantine	12.00
980.	PIN CUSHION, E.M. & Glass, removable velvet top	4.00
981.	PEN WIPER, E.M. & Glass, brush	4.00
982.	PEN WIPER, E.M. brush	4.00
983.	PEN WIPER, Metal and chamois	3.00
984.	PEN WIPER, Mosaic, chamois	12.00
985.	BLOTTER ENDS, Metal & Glass, Byzantine . . .	40.00
986.	BLOTTER CORNERS, Metal and glass, Byzantine . .	26.00
987.	BLOTTER HAND-ROLL, Metal & Glass	22.00
988.	BLOTTER ENDS, Metal Zodiac	15.00
989.	BLOTTER HAND-ROLL, Book Mark	14.00
990.	BLOTTER HAND-ROLL, Zodiac	8.00
991.	BLOTTER CORNERS, Book Mark	22.00
992.	BLOTTER ENDS, Book Mark, 12 × 19″	18.00
993.	SEAL, E.M. & Glass	4.00
995.	BLOTTER, HAND-ROLL, E.M. & Glass	8.00
996.	BLOTTER CORNERS, Zodiac, Metal	10.00
997.	BLOTTER CORNERS, E.M.	12.00
998.	BLOTTER ENDS, E.M., small, 12 × 19″	10.00
999.	BLOTTER ENDS, E.M., small, 19 × 24″	15.00
1000.	PEN TRAY, metal, Zodiac	4.00
1001.	PEN TRAY, Metal and Mosaic, swirl	5.00
1002.	PEN TRAY, E.M. & Glass, old style	6.00
1003.	PEN RACK, E.M. & Glass	5.00
1004.	PEN TRAY, E.M & Glass, new style	6.00
1006.	PAPER RACK, Metal and Glass, Byzantine	30.00
1007.	PAPER RACK, E.M. & Glass, large	25.00
1008.	PAPER RACK, E.M. & Glass, small, 10 × 6½″ . .	15.00
1009.	PAPER RACK, Metal, Zodiac	12.00
1010.	PEN HOLDER, Metal	2.00
1011.	PEN TRAY, Metal & Glass, Byzantine	18.00
1012.	PENCIL HOLDER, Metal	1.00
1013.	THERMOMETER, E.M. & Glass, 8¼ × 3¾″ . . .	12.00
1014.	THERMOMETER, Metal, Zodiac	10.00
1015.	THERMOMETER, Metal & Glass, Byzantine . . .	28.00
1018.	THERMOMETER, Book Mark	17.00
1019.	LETTER RACK, E.M. & Glass	10.00
1020.	PAPER RACK, Book Mark	25.00

1021.	ENGAGEMENT PAD, Book Mark, plain	13.00
	ENGAGEMENT PAD, With calendar	14.00
1022.	ENGAGEMENT PAD, E.M. & Glass, plain . . .	9.00
1023.	ENGAGEMENT PAD, Metal & Glass, Byzantine . .	50.00
1024.	TOBACCO JAR, F.G. metal mount	30.00
1025.	TOBACCO JAR, blown glass in wire, diam. 8" . . .	35.00
1026.	TOBACCO JAR, E.M. & Glass, bent glass	30.00
1027.	BOOK RACK, E.M. & Glass, extension	25.00
1028.	LETTER RACK, Metal and Glass, Byzantine . . .	20.00
1029.	LETTER RACK, Metal, Book Mark	15.00
1036.	WALL BRACKET, Mosaic, 19 × 21"	35.00
1037.	WALL BRACKET, Mosaic, 17 × 15"	25.00
1039.	CIGAR LIGHTER, lamp suspended	25.00
1040.	CIGAR LIGHTER and ROMAN LAMP	10.00
1041.	MATCH STAND, Zodiac	15.00
1043.	TRUMPET VASES, F.G. Metal base, small	17.00
	TRUMPET VASES, F.G. Metal base, large . . .	20.00
1055.	PEN TRAY, Book Mark	
1062.	INKSTAND, F.G. body and cover, large cast base . .	60.00
1065.	INKSTAND, single, square F.G. body, metal cover .	35.00
1066.	INKSTAND, single, round, all metal, well inside, candlestick	30.00
1067.	INKSTAND, single, round, 3-legged, jeweled, T.B. top	20.00
1068.	INKSTAND, stamp boxes, casket, double, T.B. top inside	75.00
1070.	INKSTAND, double, oval, Metal, well on each end and inside	35.00
1071.	INKSTAND, 3 wells, revolving, T.B. glass	60.00
1072.	INKSTAND, single, Zodiac, large like No. 847, round	20.00
1073.	INKSTAND, single, cone shape, T.B. & Metal, in saucer	45.00
1074.	INKSTAND, single square, T.B. jeweled on sides and top, flat top, drop wells	45.00
1080.	LETTER CLIP, Zodiac	4.00
1081.	LETTER CLIP, Byzantine	
1082.	LETTER CLIP, Book mark	
1085.	PEN BRUSHES, Zodiac	9.00
1090.	ENGAGEMENT PADS, Zodiac	10.00
1095.	PAPER KNIFE, Zodiac	4.00
1096.	PAPER KNIFE, Byzantine	8.00

1097. PAPER KNIFE, Book mark 4.00

CANDLESTICKS

1200.	1 light, root design	$ 4.00
1201.	1 light, 4-legged	7.00
1202.	1 light, drill design	4.00
1203.	1 light, leaf or feather	6.00
1204.	1 light, tall, spread base-slide	11.00
1205.	1 light, bamboo, tall	7.00
1206.	1 light, bamboo, short	7.00
1207.	1 light, universal swing, all metal	15.00
1208.	1 light, universal swing, T.B.	25.00
1209.	1 light, piano, long swing arm	60.00
1210.	1 light, plain base, large tripod, jewel top	10.00
1211.	1 light, tall tripod	14.00
1212.	1 light, 3-legged-extinguisher	6.00
1213.	1 light, plain base, tall, same as Nos. 1300, 1302, 1303	4.00
1214.	1 light, tall slide round plain base	11.00
1215.	1 light, tall round grooved base, chain extinguisher .	18.00
1216.	1 light, tall F.G., plain base	25.00
1217.	1 light, tall slide pentagon top extinguisher, screws on	11.00
1218.	1 light, short tripod, round base	6.00
1219.	1 light, F.G. body & F.G. top, short	16.00
1220.	1 light, turtle back body, square base	30.00
1221.	1 light, turtle back body, round ruffle base	30.00
1222.	1 light, 4-legged inverted cradle	4.00
1223.	1 light, F.G. balls in base and stem	30.00
1224.	1 light, cast column, 4-prong shade holder	12.00
1225.	1 light, turtle back base	15.00
1226.	1 light, light-house design, mosaic	25.00
1227.	1 light, universal swing, small F.B. balls	25.00
1228.	1 light, 3-legged spiral centre brace	8.00
1229.	1 light, root base, 5 legs, 3 prongs on each, applied orn. on stem	20.00
1230.	2 lights, bud design, oval base	8.00
1231.	2 lights, leaf design	8.00
1232.	2 lights, FLEUR-DE-LIS	12.00
1233.	2 lights, round base, heavy stem	14.00
1234.	2 lights, bud handle extinguisher	16.00

1235.	2 lights, tall slide, round plain base	12.00
1236.	2 lights, round base, heavy stem, long arm	14.00
1237.	2 lights, root base, slide extinguisher	15.00
1249.	3 lights, tall slide, round base grooved	20.00
1250.	3 lights, root base, slide	20.00
1251.	3 lights, round base, heavy stem	15.00
1252.	3 lights, long arms, round base, heavy stem	15.00
1253.	3 lights, tall slide, round plain base	13.00
1265.	4 lights, lights "in a row," extinguisher in stem . .	18.00
1266.	4 lights, round base, heavy stem, long arm extinguisher	16.00
1267.	4 lights, cast stem, flame decor., long extinguisher .	50.00
1270.	5 lights, cast stem, 4 arms, 1 in center, flame decor. .	50.00
1290.	6 lights, in a row, extinguisher on stem	24.00
1291.	6 lights, heavy cast stem, 3 2-light arms	20.00
1292.	6 lights, cast stem flame decor., long extinguisher . .	55.00
1293.	7 lights, heavy cast stem, 3 2-light arms, 1 in center .	20.00
1294.	8 lights, 4 arms, similar to No. 1295	28.00
1295.	12 lights, 4 arms, similar to No. 1290	34.00
1300.	18″ single plain base, round B.G. top	7.00
1301.	20″ single plain base, round B.G. top	7.00
1302.	18″ single plain base, long B.G. top	10.00
1303.	18″ single plain base, F.G. top	15.00
1304.	18″ single Sorg base, long B.G. top	10.00
1305.	18″ single Sorg base, round B.G. top	7.00
1306.	18″ single W.C. base, round B.G. top	15.00
1307.	18″ single W.C. base, long B.G. top	15.00
1308.	18″ single W.C. base, F.G. top	18.00
1310.	13″ and 14″ single plain base, round B.G. top . . .	7.00
1312.	Single tripod, long B.G. top	7.00
1313.	Double swing arm, scalloped base	15.00
1315.	4 lights, jeweled base, round B.G. top	20.00
1316.	2 lights, jeweled base, round B.G. top	15.00
1318.	WILD CARROT, natural flower, plain base 8.00, 10.00, 12.00	
1319.	WILD CARROT, natural flower, W.C. base 10.00, 12.00, 15.00	
1320.	WILD CARROT, natural flower, bead rim base 8.00, 10.00, 12.00	
1322.	15″ single scalloped base, pineapple top B.G. . . .	15.00
1323.	18″ single scalloped base, pineapple top B.G. . . .	15.00
1324.	15″ single plain base, pineapple top B.G.	12.00

1325.	18″ single plain base, pineapple top B.G.	12.00
1327.	Miniature candlestick desk	2.00
1328.	1 light, B.G. pineapple round plain base, base like No. 1210	12.00
1331.	18″ SAXIFRAGE	20.00
1332.	18″ TULIP TREE	20.00
1333.	SNAKE, adjustable, for F.G. globe, wrought . . .	8.00
1361.	Candle lamp, F.G. and F.G. globe metal mount (comp.)	35.00
1362.	Candle lamp and shade, B.G., in metal, 17″ high (comp.)	40.00
1363.	Candle lamp, metal, bamboo design	15.00

LEADED SHADES

1400.	10″ VINE BORDER, plain squares, dome	$25.00
1402.	5¼″ Candleshade, etched metal and silk, mica lined, cone	3.00
1404.	10″ AZALEA, dome	40.00
1410.	12″ VINE BORDER, plain squares, dome	25.00
1411.	12″ Plain squares, or brick dome	20.00
1414.	12″ APPLE BLOSSOM, dome	50.00
1416.	12″ Shell shade, dome	40.00
1417.	12″ DOGWOOD, dome	60.00
1418.	14″ ARROW HEAD, high cone	70.00
1419.	14″ Plain squares, Turtle Back Band, dome . . .	45.00
1420.	14″ VINE BORDER, Plain squares, dome	30.00
1421.	14″ Plain Squares, or brick, dome	25.00
1423.	14″ WOODBINE, dome	40.00
1425.	14″ Shell shade, dome	45.00
1426.	14″ DAFFODIL, dome	60.00
1427.	14″ DAFFODIL, high cone	60.00
1429.	16″ Fern shade, dome	75.00
1430.	16″ Indian design, dome	35.00
1432.	16″ Shell shade, dome	50.00
1434.	16″ Plain squares, Turtle Back Band, dome . . .	50.00
1435.	16″ VINE BORDER, plain squares, dome	35.00
1436.	16″ Plain Squares, or brick, dome	30.00
1437.	16″ TREFOIL BORDER, plain squares, dome . . .	35.00
1438.	16″ COLONIAL, dome	40.00

1439.	16″ FEATHER JEWELED, dome	30.00
1440.	16″ RIBBON DECORATION, waved, dome . . .	35.00
1442.	16″ FISH, FLYING, dome	100.00
1443.	16″ BAMBOO, dome	80.00
1444.	16″ GREEK BORDER, dome	55.00
1445.	16″ VINE ORNAMENT, plain squares, dome . . .	45.00
1446.	16″ DOGWOOD, dome	85.00
1447.	16″ BLACK-EYED-SUSAN, dome	85.00
1448.	16″ PANSY, dome	90.00
1449.	16″ DAFFODIL, dome	75.00
1450.	16″ MUSHROOM, dome	60.00
1451.	16″ GERANIUM, cone	90.00
1454.	16″ TULIP CLUSTER, dome	75.00
1455.	16″ APPLE BLOSSOM, dome	75.00
1456.	16″ Irregular tulip, dome	65.00
1457.	16″ POMEGRANATE, dome, plain squares . . .	35.00
1458.	16″ POPPY, conventional dome	65.00
1459.	16″ PEBBLE, dome	100.00
1460.	16″ FISH AND WATER, cone	100.00
1461.	16″ POPPY, cone	85.00
1462.	16″ DRAGON FLY, cone	80.00
1463.	16″ NASTURTIUM, lattice, irregular edge, wave . .	75.00
1464.	16″ PEACOCK, dome	90.00
1465.	16″ YELLOW ROSE AND BUTTERFLY, honey-comb, dome	80.00
1468.	16″ WOODBINE, dome	55.00
1469.	18″ Plain Squares, or brick, low dome	45.00
1470.	18″ VINE BORDER, plain squares, low dome . . .	50.00
1471.	18″ CRESCENT BORDER, plain squares, low dome .	50.00
1472.	18″ PEACOCK, low dome	115.00
1473.	18″ TYLER, GREEK SCROLL	100.00
1474.	18″ VINE ORNAMENT, plain squares, low dome .	60.00
1475.	18″ PEONY, Tyler	125.00
1476.	18″ Geometrical straight lines for No. 439, Holden .	75.00
1477.	18″ IRREGULAR POPPY, Tyler	100.00
1478.	18″ DOGWOOD, low dome	115.00
1479.	18″ ALLAMANDA, flat	65.00
1480.	18″ CLEMATIS, flat	65.00
1481.	18″ NASTURTIUM, low dome	100.00
1482.	18″ Plain Squares, Turtle Back Band, dome	75.00
1483.	18″ TULIP TREE, flat	65.00

1484. 20" Plain squares, Turtle Back Band, cone 100.00
1485. 18" Straight panels, Favrile glass balls around edge,
            for 437 cone 35.00
1486. 18" GENTIAN BLOSSOM, convential [*sic*] jeweled,
            flat 100.00
1487. 20" Plain squares, Turtle Back Band, dome 100.00
1488. 18" VINE BORDER, dome 45.00
1490. 20" POND LILY, cone 115.00
1491. 20" DOGWOOD, band 115.00
1492. 20" NASTURTIUM, low dome 125.00
1493. 20" Plain squares, or brick, cone, shape of 1496 . . 40.00
1494. 20" VINE BORDER, plain squares, dome 60.00
1495. 20" DRAGONFLY, cone 90.00
1496. 20" ARROWHEAD, cone 100.00
1497. 20" DAFFODIL, cone 100.00
1498. 20" VINE BORDER, plain squares, Holden . . . 60.00
1499. 21" CLEMATIS, cone 100.00
1501. 22" Plain squares, O'Brien 75.00
1502. 20" LILY PADS, for No. 443, flat 100.00
1503. 22" Turtle Back Band (high band), Holden . . . 100.00
1504. 22" DOGWOOD, Holden 140.00
1505. 22" PEONY, Holden 150.00
1506. 22" NASTURTIUM, Holden 140.00
1507. 22" DRAGONFLY, Holden 175.00
1508. 22" Plain squares, Favrile glass ball border, dome . . 100.00
1509. 22" BAMBOO, dome 150.00
1510. 24" VINE BORDER, plain squares, dome 100.00
1511. 22" Turtle Back Band, band on lower edge 115.00
1512. 22" APPLE BLOSSOM, O'Brien 200.00
1513. 22" Plain squares, cast leaf border with Favrile glass
            balls, low dome 100.00
1514. 22" Plain squares, flat 75.00
1515. 24" Conventional, dome 100.00
1516. 24" Plain squares, flat 90.00
1517. 22" Plain Squares, high dome 75.00
1518. 25" BLACK-EYED-SUSAN, like shade of No. 351 . 300.00
1520. 24" Plain Square, Williams 50.00
1521. 24" BAMBOO, dome 200.00
1522. 24" GOURD, cone . . . .
1523. 25" Gillespie, plain squares, flat 65.00
1524. 25" LOTUS, Pagoda 125.00

1526.	26" FISH SCALE, high dome	150.00
1530.	20" APPLE BLOSSOM, dome	175.00
1531.	20" POPPY, DRAGONFLY block, cone	115.00
1532.	20" Plain squares, Beckley, narrow T.B. border on lower edge	85.00
1533.	18" NASTURTIUM on No. 1475 Block	
1537.	24" LABURNUM, No. 1538 Block	225.00
1538.	24" SNOWBALL, irregular edge	200.00
1539.	22" LABURNUM, for No. 367	175.00
1540.	10" Plain, squares, ball	30.00
1543.	PEONY, elaborate, 6½ × 10½	90.00
1544.	10" DOGWOOD, ball	90.00
1545.	GLOBE, conventional, inverted	30.00
1546.	10" BALL, AUTUMN LEAVES	75.00
1560.	14" IRREGULAR TULIP, dome	60.00
1561.	14" POMEGRANATE, BORDER, plain squares, dome	30.00
1562.	14" GERANIUM	65.00
1565.	10" Hexagon, straight panels, Turtle Back glass on top for No. 434 lamp	12.00
1567.	12" Conventional, round and chip jewels, cone, for No. 461 lamp	
1568.	10" Plain squares	20.00
1570.	16" Pressed Jeweled border, plain squares, dome . .	50.00
1571.	16" SNOWBALL, irregular edge, dome	100.00
1572.	16" Plain squares, Favrile glass ball band	65.00
1573.	16" DOGWOOD, on No. 1442 block	75.00
1580.	Etched metal candleshade, dome, to cover glass shades	4.00
1581.	Etched metal candleshade, cone, to cover glass shades	3.00

CANDLESTICK TOPS

A.	All metal tripod	$1.00
B.	Jewel	2.00
C.	Poppy B.G. in metal, round	3.00
D.	Long B.G. in metal	5.00
E.	F.G. Short	3.00
F.	Magnolia B.G. in metal	5.00
G.	F.G. long, pear shape	6.00
H.	F.G. long, pear shape, extra long	8.00

I.   Low squat B.G. in metal similar to "C" .   .   .   3.00
J.   Extra long B.G. in metal 7.00
K.   Pineapple, B.G. in metal 5.00
L.   Cast all metal with 7″ holder .   .   .   .   .   .

APPENDIX 2

TIFFANY STUDIOS PHOTO CATALOGUE *

85 Original Photos of Lamps and Shades
Made at Tiffany Studios, New York,
with a Price List of 1933
and Tiffany Model Numbers

---

* Actually, a looseleaf notebook consisting of a series of pages with photographs and prices in numerical order that was used at Tiffany Studios as a reference book for their salesmen.

Item	Base #	Price	Shade #		Price	Total Cost
1.	306	$ 36	104	3@	$ 2.50	$ 43.50
2.	318	68	1410		40.00	108.00
3.	337	50	1424		65.00	115.00
4.	356	140	1585		80.00	120.00
5.	367	155	1501		75.00	230.00
6.	368	100	1549		125.00	225.00
7.	375	200	1597		400.00	600.00
8.	376	225	1902		425.00	650.00
9.	377	165	1515		150.00	210.00
10.	379	155	1903		275.00	420.00
11.	381	100	104	10@	2.50	125.00
12.	382	110	104	12@	2.50	140.00
13.	383	150	104	18@	2.50	195.00
14.	385	90	104	7@	2.50	107.50
15.	387	110	1539		350.00	460.00
16.	397	175	1907		120.00	295.00
17.	413		Complete			70.00
18.	414		Complete			70.00
19.	415	60	10″		14.00	74.00
20.	416	45	7″		8.00	53.00
21.	417	50	7″		8.00	58.00
22.	418	32	1940A		30.00	62.00
23.	419	37	7″		8.00	45.00
24.	423	62	1409		30.00	92.00
25.	423H	75	12″		19.00	94.00
26.	424	42	7″		8.00	50.00
27.	425	75	10″		14.00	89.00
28.	426	30	7″		8.00	38.00
29.	429A	45	Silk		———	45.00+
30.	430	300	1936		40.00	340.00
31.	432	275	1936		40.00	315.00

1

2

Item	Base #	Price	Shade #	Price	Total Cost
32.	515		Complete		$ 250.00
33.	528	65	1493	$ 75.00	140.00
34.	529	100	1907	120.00	220.00
35.	533	45	1900	45.00	90.00
36.	534	45	1901	45.00	90.00
37.	535	45	1588	35.00	80.00
38.	536	30	1587	30.00	60.00
39.	538	50	1413	45.00	95.00
40.	539	50	1412	45.00	95.00
41.	541		Complete		75.00
42.	550	200	1507	200.00	400.00
43.	552		Complete		38.00
44.	553	80	1537	400.00	480.00
45.	554	45	1426	90.00	135.00
46.	556		Complete		60.00
47.	557	80	1953	300.00	380.00
48.	558	45	1411	35.00	80.00
49.	561	40	1950	65.00	105.00
50.	569	55	1409	30.00	85.00
51.	576	165	1408	30.00	195.00
52.	582	115	10″	14.00	129.00
53.	584	50	1467	100.00	150.00
54.	585	55	1913	55.00	110.00
55.	587	75	1927	90.00	165.00
56.	590	45	8″	11.50	56.50
57.	604	75	1928	50.00	125.00
58.	606	30	7″	8.00	38.00
59.	608	30	8″	11.50	41.50
60.	612	38	1937	45.00	83.00
61.	613	45	1938	32.00	77.00
62.	614	35	1924	18.00	53.00
63.	616	38	10″	14.00	52.00
64.	617	38	12″	19.00	57.00
65.	618	35	10″	14.00	49.00
66.	627	90	1927	90.00	180.00
67.	628	110	1469	60.00	170.00
68.	629	110	1469	60.00	170.00
69.	660	175	Silk		175.00
70.	661	37	7″	8.00	45.00

3

4

Item	Base #	Price	Shade #		Price	Total Cost
71.	662	Complete parchment shade				$ 140.00
72.	663	Complete				225.00
73.	664	42	7"		$ 8.00	50.00
74.	665	37	7"		8.00	45.00
75.	Shade Only	1491	Diam. 20"			175.00
76.	Shade Only	1495	Diam. 20"			130.00
77.	Shade Only	1915	Diam. 26"			200.00
78.	Shade Only	1916	Diam. 20"			95.00
79.	Shade Only	1917	Diam. 20"			160.00
80.	Shade Only	1918	Diam. 20"			175.00
81.	Shade Only	1515	Diam. 24"			150.00
82.	Shade Only	1531	Diam. 20"			175.00
83.	Shade Only	1497	Diam. 20"			140.00
84.	Shade Only	1524	Diam. 25"			150.00
85.	Shade Only	1539	Diam. 24"			400.00

5

6

7

8

9

10

11

12

13

14

15

16

17

19

20

18

24

21

22

23

25

26

27

28

29

30

31

32

33

34

35

36

37

38

39

40

41

42

43

44

45

46

47

48

49

50

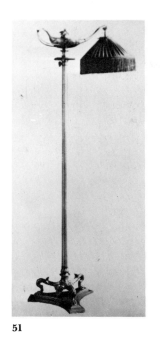

51

52

53

54

55

56

57

58

59

60

61

62

63

64

65

66

67

68

69

70

71

72

73

74

75

76

77

78

80

79

82

81

83

84

85

INDEX

Italic numerals refer to page numbers of illustrations or captions.